BC Science CONNECTIONS 8
Student Workbook

Development Team

Lionel Sandner
Senior Program Consultant
Victoria, BC

Van Chau
Delview Secondary School
Delta School District #37

Grace Lai
District Education Centre
Surrey School District #36

Shelagh Lim
Cambridge Elementary
Surrey School District #36

Delyth Morgan
Royal Oak Middle School
Saanich School District #63

John Munro
Rick Hansen Secondary School of Science and Business
Abbotsford School District #34

James Stewart
J.A. Hutton School
Boundary School District #51

NELSON

NELSON

BC Science Connections 8 Student Workbook

ISBN 13: 978-1-25-965143-4
ISBN 10: 1-25-965143-6

6 7 8 9   22 21 20 19

Printed and bound in the United States

DIRECTOR LEARNING SOLUTIONS & PRODUCT DEVELOPMENT (K-12): Lenore Brooks
PUBLISHER: Jean Ford
SENIOR CONTENT MANAGER: Jonathan Bocknek
SUBJECT MATTER EXPERTS/DEVELOPMENTAL EDITORS: Christine Weber, Christine Arnold, Gurmeet Sodhi-Bains
SUPERVISING EDITOR: Shannon Martin
COPY EDITORS: Kelli Howey
EDITORIAL ASSISTANT: Erin Hartley
PRODUCTION COORDINATOR: Sarah Strynatka
INTERIOR DESIGN: Brian Lehen Graphic Design Ltd.
COVER DESIGN: Vince Satira
ELECTRONIC PAGE MAKE-UP: Brian Lehen Graphic Design Ltd.

COVER IMAGES: Background: Connor Stephanson; Band Images: left, Greg Epperson/Shutterstock; Myvisuals/Shutterstock; Panos Karas/Shutterstock; lightpoet/Shutterstock; photo courtesy of the Bridge River Indian Band, photographer Betty Weaver, used by permission of Mr. Gerald Michell; Masterfile

Contents

Safety Concepts   vi

Science Safety Symbols   viii

Safety Observations   ix

How Safe Am I?   x

Unit 1 Life processes are performed at the cellular level

Topic 1.1   What are the characteristics of living things?   2
            Communicating: Living Versus Non-Living   3
            Processing and Analyzing: Characteristics of Living Things   4
            Evaluating: Interdependent Characteristics   5
            Applying and Innovating: Investigating Growth and Development   6
            1.1 Assessment   7

Topic 1.2   Where do living things come from?   10
            Processing and Analyzing: Cell Theory   11
            Communicating: Comparing a Cell to a Virus   12
            Evaluating: Are Viruses Alive?   13
            1.2 Assessment   14

Topic 1.3   How are cells different from one another?   17
            Communicating: Prokaryotic and Eukaryotic Cells   19
            Evaluating: The Function of Cell Structures   20
            Applying and Innovating: A Plant Cell is Like a Shopping Mall   21
            Planning and Conducting: Rate of Photosynthesis   22
            1.3 Assessment   24

Topic 1.4   What interactions occur between humans and micro-organisms   27
            Applying and Innovating: How Small Are Microbes?   28
            Evaluating: Roles of Microbes   30
            Communicating: Useful Microbes   31
            Processing and Analyzing: Pathogens That Cause Food Poisoning   32
            1.4 Assessment   34

Topic 1.5   How does the body protect us from pathogens?   37
            Applying and Innovating: The First Line of Defence   38
            Evaluating: The Body's Lines of Defence   39
            Questioning and Predicting: Flu Season   40
            Applying and Innovating: Epidemic, Outbreak, and Pandemic   42
            1.5 Assessment   43

Topic 1.6   What medicines help protect us from microbes that make us sick?   46
            Applying and Innovating: Traditional Plant Medicines   47
            Communicating: How Vaccines and Antibiotics Work   48
            Evaluating: Types of Vaccines   49
            Processing and Analyzing: How Effective are Vaccines?   50
            1.6 Assessment   52

Unit 1 AT Issue: What is the world's deadliest animal?   55

Unit 2 The behavior of matter can be explained by the kinetic molecular theory and atomic theory

Topic 2.1 How does matter affect your life?   58
           Communicating: Identifying Hazardous Household Products Symbols   59
           Applying and Innovating: Understanding WHMIS and HHPS   60
           Evaluating: Safety Do's and Don'ts   61
           2.1 Assessment   62

Topic 2.2 What are some ways to describe matter?   66
           Questioning and Predicting: Creating a Density Tower   68
           Processing and Analyzing: Density of Different Objects   69
           Planning and Conducting: Identifying Substances Based on Physical Properties   70
           Applying and Innovating: Physical and Chemical Changes   71
           Applying and Innovating: Mixture or Pure Substance?   73
           2.2 Assessment   74

Topic 2.3 How can we describe and explain the states of matter?   78
           Applying and Innovating: Visualizing the Kinetic Molecular Theory   79
           Communicating: Properties of the States of Matter   80
           Evaluating: Changes of State   81
           Processing and Analyzing: Changes of State of Silver   82
           Planning and Conducting: Effects of Temperature on Diffusion   83
           2.3 Assessment   84

Topic 2.4 How can we investigate and explain the composition of atoms?   88
           Applying and Innovating: Atomic Theory Timeline   90
           Planning and Conducting: Rutherford's Gold Foil Experiment   91
           Processing and Analyzing: Parts of an Atom   92
           Communicating: Quarks and Leptons   93
           2.4 Assessment   94

Unit 2 AT Issue: What do engineers have to take into account when building a bridge?   98

Unit 3 Energy can be transferred as both a particle and a wave

Topic 3.1 How does electromagnetic radiation shape your world?   100
           Communicating: Electromagnetic Radiation Applications   102
           Processing and Analyzing: How Does Electromagnetic Radiation Shape
               Your World?   103
           Processing and Analyzing: Using Electromagnetic Radiation to See Our World   104
           Evaluating: Electromagnetic Radiation: Plus, Minus, and Interesting   105
           3.1 Assessment   106

Topic 3.2 How can models explain the properties of electromagnetic radiation?   109
           Communicating: Making Sense of Models   111
           Processing and Analyzing: Young's Experiment   112
           Communicating: Parts of a Wave   113
           Processing and Analyzing: Characteristics of Waves   114
           Applying and Innovating: Another Thought Experiment   115
           3.2 Assessment   117

Topic 3.3   How does light behave when it encounters different materials and surfaces?   120
        Communicating: Classifying Materials   122
        Processing and Analyzing: How Light Behaves   123
        3.3 Assessment   124

Topic 3.4   How does light behave when it is reflected?   126
        Planning and Conducting: Practice with Protractors   128
        Evaluating: How Do the Images Formed in Mirrors Compare?   129
        Processing and Analyzing: Looking into Mirrors   130
        3.4 Assessment   131

Topic 3.5   How does light behave when it moves from one medium to another?   134
        Processing and Analyzing: Diverging and Converging Lenses   136
        Processing and Analyzing: The Parts of the Eye?   137
        Applying and Innovating: An Optical Device to Improve Eyesight   138
        Communicating: Putting the Terms Together   139
        3.5 Assessment   140

Unit 3 AT Issue: What do we need to know about blue light?   143

Unit 4   The theory of plate tectonics explains Earth's geological processes

Topic 4.1   What ideas, observations, and evidence led to the theory of plate tectonics?   144
        Evaluating: Considering Evidence for Continental Drift   145
        Processing and Analyzing: Layers of Earth   148
        Applying and Innovating: Sea Floor Spreading   149
        4.1 Assessment   150

Topic 4.2   What are tectonic plates and how is their movement linked to geological processes?   153
        Communicating: The Lithosphere and Asthenosphere   154
        Processing and Analyzing: Plate Boundaries   155
        Planning and Conducting: Mantle Convection   156
        4.2 Assessment   157

Topic 4.3   How does the theory of plate tectonics explain Earth's geological processes?   161
        Applying and Innovating: At the Surface: Before and After   163
        Applying and Innovating: Interpreting Epicentres of the Juan de Fuca Plate   164
        Communicating: Volcanoes at Convergent Boundaries   165
        Applying and Innovating: Volcanic Ash Analysis   166
        Evaluating: Mountain Ranges   167
        4.3 Assessment   168

Topic 4.4   How do geological features and processes affect where and how we live?   172
        Applying and Innovating: Being Prepared   173
        Applying and Innovating: Geohazards in British Columbia   174
        Applying and Innovating: The Geology of Your Region   175
        4.4 Assessment   176

Unit 4 AT Issue: Should we worry about the Cascadia subduction zone?   178

Safety Concepts

Use with textbook pages xiv-xvii.

Safety in your science class means knowing how to apply the safety rules, practicing safe lab procedures, and following your teacher's instructions. Safety is a way of thinking and acting. It involves how you behave with the equipment you use and the people you work with.

As you read each section, draw what you "See" or what you "Hear" in your head.

Draw What you "See or Hear"	Rules and Procedures
1. General rules 	• Listen to and read all instructions. • Ask questions if you do not understand a step. • Identify the safety symbols and precautions in an experiment. ● Know where to find and how to use the eye wash station, emergency deluge shower, fire extinguisher, fire blanket, and fire alarm. ● Tell your teacher about allergies or anything else that could stop you from hearing, seeing, or doing the lab. • Wait for your teacher's permission to start working on any activity or investigation.
2. Acting responsibly 	• Wear safety equipment such as goggles, gloves, and a lab apron as instructed by your teacher. • Tie back long hair, loose clothing, and dangling jewelry. • Never chew gum, eat, or drink in the science classroom. Do not taste or put anything in your mouth. • Carefully handle equipment. ● Tell your teacher if something is not safe, especially if it is a chemical spill, broken equipment, or someone behaving unsafely. ● Listen as the teacher describes all the safety issues and where to put waste materials. • Wash your hands before and after you handle any equipment and materials in investigations. • Clean up your workstation, return materials, equipment, and waste to the appropriate locations as directed by your teacher.
3. Working with sharp objects 	• When cutting, move the scissors or the knife away from your body. • Keep safety guards on scalpels or any sharp tools until they are to be used. ● When walking with sharp objects, like scissors or scalpels, carry them with pointed end downward, away from you and others. ● Tell the teacher if the equipment is broken and has a sharp edge. Be careful with it. • Ask the teacher where to put broken glass.

Draw What you "See or Hear"	Rules and Procedures
4. Working with electrical equipment	• Dry your hands before touching electrical cords, plugs, or sockets. • Pull the plug, not the cord, when unplugging electrical equipment. • Tell the teacher if the electrical equipment is damaged. • Keep electrical cords away from where people walk.
5. Working with heat *Oh, its cool. lets grab it! ou! OW! HOODH*	• Always use heat-proof containers such as Pyrex® glassware. • Stay with the object as it is heated. Never leave heating objects unattended. • Point the end of a container being heated away from you and others. • Do not let a container boil dry. • Listen to your teacher explain how to safely light and use a Bunsen burner. • Hot objects do not look hot and they will burn you! Handle hot plates carefully. • If you burn yourself, immediately run cold water on the burn and tell your teacher.
6. Working with chemicals	• If a chemical spills on your... **Body** – Wash with water immediately at the closest emergency deluge shower station and tell your teacher! **Eyes** – Wash immediately at the closest eye wash station for minimum of 15 min. Tell your teacher! **Desk** – Don't touch it! Ask your teacher how to clean it up safely. • When smelling a substance, fan or "waft" the fumes toward you. Never smell directly from a bottle! • When pouring chemicals, keep your face away from the container.
7. Designing and building	• Use the right tool for the job and handle the tools with care. • Read the instructions for using modelling clay. Wash your hands when done. • Read the operating instructions when using mechanical equipment. • Carefully observe and work with moving objects. Tie back loose hair and clothing.

Highlight one or two rules in each section that you think are the most important.
Why did you think they were important?

1. You could get acid in your eyes. 2. Someone could step on the glass. 3. You could stab someone. 4. You could eletricute your-self. 5. Someone could touch it and get burnt. 6. It could be poisonous. 7. You could breath it.

Safety Concepts **vii**

Science Safety Symbols

Use with textbook pages xv and 97-101.

In 2015, Canada updated its method of identifying dangerous materials in the workplace. The new **Workplace Hazardous Materials Information System** (WHMIS) closely follows the United Nations' labelling system called the Globally Harmonized System of Classification and Labelling of Chemicals (GHS). Each chemical also has a Safety Data Sheet (SDS) that gives more detailed information on how the chemical reacts, how it should be stored, and what to do if an accident occurs.

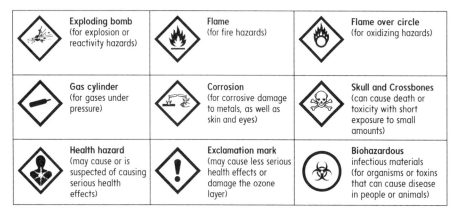

Canada also uses the **Hazardous Household Products Symbols** (HHPS) for items you would use in your home such as hair spray, oven cleaner, and bleach. It was also updated and simplified from the old HHPS system.

Draw a WHMIS and HHPS Venn Diagram to compare and contrast the two systems.

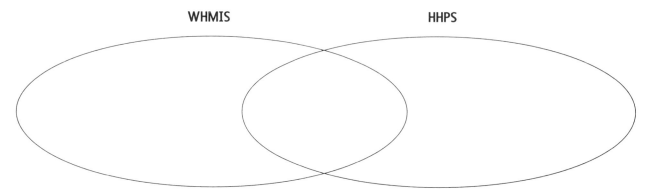

Safety Observations

Use with textbook pages xiv–xvii.

There are many safety problems in the science lab shown below. Highlight as many as you can.

Choose six of the problems you understand the best and number them 1 to 6 on the diagram. For each of the 6 problems, describe what the safety problem is, why it is a problem, and what should be done to fix it.

What is the Problem?	Why is it a Problem?	How to Fix the Problem
1.		
2.		
3.		
4.		
5.		
6.		

How Safe Am I?

Use with textbook pages xiv–xvii.

Each of the following situations could happen in a science classroom.

1. Someone sneezed just as your teacher was telling you about a lab chemical. You read the label, but it was old and partially worn off.

   a) Draw the WHMIS symbols that should be on the label.

   > **Phenolphthalein solution**
   > Avoid contact with eyes and lungs.
   > Will cause irritation of respiratory tract.
   > Reproductive toxin. If swallowed, contact doctor immediately. Flammable near an open flame.

   b) List all the safety equipment you should use.

   _____

   _____

   c) If you accidentally spill this chemical on your hand, what should you do?

   _____

   _____

   _____

2. Two classmates at your lab station are putting on lipstick and eye shadow.

   a) Is this a safety concern for the class? Explain.

   _____

   _____

   b) What should you do and why?

   _____

   _____

3. You arrive late to the lab and missed both the lab demonstration and safety talk. Your lab partner is absent and your science binder is in the art class. Since you were the last person to pick up equipment, you were left with two chipped beakers and a broken hot plate.

a) Are *you* a safety concern for the class? Explain.

_____

_____

_____

b) What 2 things should you do immediately?

_____

_____

_____

c) What 3 things should you do for future labs?

_____

_____

_____

4. Hot water is about to boil over on your neighbour's hot plate.

a) Is this a safety concern for the class? Explain.

_____

_____

_____

b) What should you do and why?

_____

_____

_____

What are the characteristics of living things?

Use with textbook pages 6–13.

 *Check for Understanding*

As you read this section, highlight any words or sentences that help you develop your understanding.

Reading Check

What makes something a living thing?

_____

_____

_____

_____

Living or Non-living?

Scientists distinguish between things they consider to be living and things they consider to be non-living. Scientists have come up with a list of characteristics that all living things have in common. To decide whether a thing is living or non-living, scientists judge the thing against the set of characteristics.

To be considered living, a thing must have all the characteristics of life. If even just one characteristic is missing, the thing is judged to be non-living.

Characteristics of Living Things

Characteristic	Comments
Living things are made of cells.	• Some living things are a single cell. • Some living things have many cells.
Living things take in nutrients.	• Animals and most other living things get nutrients from food by eating other living things. • Green plants and plant-like organisms make their own food.
Living things use energy.	• Some nutrients in food are used to provide energy that is needed to live and function.
Living things produce wastes.	• When living things use nutrients, they produce wastes such as carbon dioxide, urine, and feces. • Wastes can cause harm, so they must be removed from cells and/or the body.
Living things respond to stimuli.	• Stimuli is the plural of stimulus. A stimulus is anything that causes a reaction or response. • If you are itchy (*stimulus*), you scratch the itch (*response*). If you are tired (*stimulus*), you rest (*response*). If you think something is funny (*stimulus*), you laugh (*response*).
Living things grow.	• "Grow" can mean increasing in size or increasing the number of cells in the body.
Living things reproduce.	• Living things make more of their own kind (species) by reproducing. • Reproduction is not needed for individual living things to survive. Reproduction ensures that the species—the kind of organism a living thing is—will continue to survive.

Living Versus Non-Living

Use with textbook pages 8–11.

1. What distinguishes a living thing from a non-living thing? Some non-living things have some of the same characteristics as living things. Consider a firefly and a fire. Compare and contrast these two things, noting their similarities and their differences in characteristics. Fill in the following Compare and Contrast Graphic Organizer that has been partially completed for you.

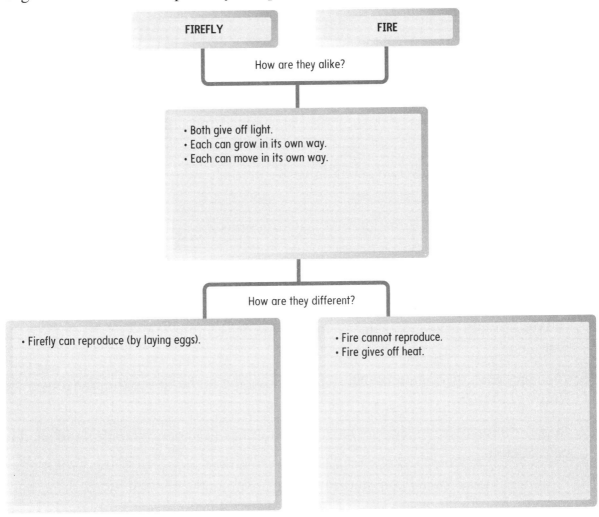

FIREFLY   FIRE

How are they alike?

- Both give off light.
- Each can grow in its own way.
- Each can move in its own way.

How are they different?

- Firefly can reproduce (by laying eggs).

- Fire cannot reproduce.
- Fire gives off heat.

2. Explain why one is considered to be living, while the other is considered to be non-living.

A firefly eats and reproduces as fire dosent eat, fireflys are produced and fire is made.

Characteristics of Living Things

Use with textbook pages 8-11.

Identify the characteristic of living things described in each statement. A list of the characteristics is given below.

A. reproduce	E. take in nutrients
B. use energy	F. respond to stimuli
C. made of cells	G. grow and develop
D. produce waste	

1. A tadpole undergoes metamorphosis and becomes a bullfrog. _____G_____

2. Humans breathe out carbon dioxide when they exhale. _____D_____

3. Birds produce guano as a thick white paste consisting of mostly uric acid. _____D_____

4. A bacterium splits into two equal halves to produce two new daughter cells. _____A_____

5. Under a microscope, some internal leaf structures are arranged like bricks in a wall. _____C_____

6. A raft of Steller sea lions consume fish, squid, and octopus as part of their diet. _____E_____

7. A Western rattlesnake coils up on the road to bask in the sun so that it can stay warm. _____F_____

8. A runner eats a spaghetti dinner to carbo-load the night before the Vancouver Sun Run. _____E_____

9. In order to increase in size, a Dungeness crab has to undergo moulting to shed its exoskeleton. _____G_____

10. A student views *Euglena*, a unicellular organism, under the microscope and makes a sketch of it in her notebook. _____C_____

11. Thousands of spawning salmon can be seen swimming upstream along the Adams River in Kamloops to lay and fertilize their eggs. _____A_____

12. The European wall lizards on the Saanich Peninsula eat lots of insects to have enough energy for their active lifestyle jumping. _____B_____

Interdependent Characteristics

Use with textbook pages 8–11.

Identify two characteristics of living things that are interdependent because they are closely related in each scenario described below.

1. Sunflowers are known to follow and face the Sun as they grow.

   _____

2. The body produces new skin cells through cell division to help seal a wound from a cut.

   _____

3. A sunflower sea star has the ability to regenerate a lost arm and regrow another one.

   _____

4. A black-tailed deer fawn doubles in weight after suckling milk from its mother for the first two weeks of its life.

   _____

5. A black bear will eat large quantities of salmon and berries to store up body fat before it hibernates for the winter.

   _____

6. When red blood cells reach the lungs, carbon dioxide molecules diffuse out of blood cells into the air sacs for exhalation.

   _____

7. As a spider crawls along the leaf of a Venus flytrap, it triggers the hair on the leaf, which causes the trap to snap shut. The plant then digests the spider.

   _____

8. A tree absorbs nutrients and water from the soil, takes in carbon dioxide from the atmosphere, and captures the Sun's energy to produce food and oxygen through the process of photosynthesis.

   _____

Investigating Growth and Development

Use with textbook pages 9.

Will adding nitrogen fertilizer to soil affect the growth and development of radish plants? Two students designed an experiment to find out. They got three pots to grow the seeds. Each pot got 400 mL of potting soil from the same bag.

a) They added 2 g of fertilizer to the soil of one pot and labelled it Pot A.

b) They added 4 g of fertilizer to the soil of a second pot and labelled it Pot B.

c) They added 6 g of fertilizer to the soil of a third pot and labelled it Pot C.

Five radish seeds were placed at the same depth in each pot. All the pots were exposed to the same amount of sunlight and given the same amount of water for 6 days. They measured and recorded the height of the tallest seedling in each pot each day.

Data Table

Day	Height of Tallest Seedling (mm) in Pot A	Height of Tallest Seedling (mm) in Pot B	Height of Tallest Seedling (mm) in Pot C
1	0	0	0
2	3	5	7
3	6	10	16
4	9	16	26
5	12	23	38
6	15	30	60

1. If the students were to create a graph to display the data, what variable would be placed on the *x*-axis? What would be placed on the *y*-axis?

_____

2. State the hypothesis being investigated for this experiment.

_____

3. What variables were kept the same in this experiment?

_____

4. Identify an error in the experimental design.

_____

5. What must the students do for their results to be considered valid?

_____

1.1 Assessment

Match each term on the left with the best description on the right. Each description may be used only once.

Term	Description
1. _____ cell	A. the basic unit of life
2. _____ producer	B. an organism made up of one cell
3. _____ consumer	C. an organism made up of many cells
4. _____ internal stimulus	D. an organism that must eat other organisms to get nutrients
5. _____ external stimulus	E. has the ability to produce its own food using the Sun's energy
6. _____ unicellular organism	F. something from inside an organism that causes the organism to respond
7. _____ multicellular organism	G. a change from the external environment that causes an organism to respond

Circle the letter of the best answer for questions 8 to 16.

8. Which of the following organisms relies on other organisms for energy and nutrients?

   A. moss   **C.** apple tree

   B. algae   **D.** snowy owl

9. Which of the following terms is incorrectly paired with the example?

   A. unicellular organism—head louse

   B. producer—Western Red Cedar tree

   C. consumer—Vancouver Island marmot

   D. multicellular organism—Pacific Dogwood tree

10. Hunger and thirst are two examples of

   A. life processes   **C.** external stimuli

   B. internal stimuli   **D.** sources of energy

11. Which of the following is an example of an external stimulus?

   A. An athlete starts to sweat to cool down.

   B. A student starts to feel sleepy after a long day.

   C. A student notices his heart rate goes up after climbing a flight of stairs.

   D. A geranium plant does not have a lot of starch stored in its leaves after being placed in a dark room for several days.

12. Which of the following scenarios are examples of "response to a stimulus"?

I	*Euglena* excretes water and waste through a vacuole.
II	The leaves of a sleepy plant shrink when they are touched.
III	*Paramecium* moves away from the cooler water toward the warmer water.

   A. I and II only

   B. I and III only

   C. II and III only

   D. I, II, and III

13. A female frog can release up to 4000 eggs at one time during mating season. What characteristics of life are described by this statement?

I	Living things reproduce.
II	Living things use energy.
III	Living things produce waste products.

   A. I and II only

   B. I and III only

   C. II and III only

   D. I, II, and III

14. A grasshopper sheds its exoskeleton through moulting in order to increase in size. With what characteristic of living things would moulting be associated?

   A. reproduction

   B. made of cells

   C. producing waste

   D. growth and development

15. A conservation officer points out some black bear scat (droppings) to a group of students. Bear scat is associated with which two characteristics of living things?

   A. using energy and reproduction

   B. reproduction and response to stimuli

   C. taking in nutrients and producing waste

   D. growth and development and made of cells

16. A student wanted to carry out an experiment using pea seeds to see the effects of different environmental factors on rate of plant growth over several weeks. Which of the following factors would not be considered a variable in this experiment?

A. light intensity

B. soil temperature

C. type of pea seeds

D. amount of road salt added to the soil

17. Complete the T-chart to compare and contrast **"From what do living things get their energy?"** and **"For what do living things use the energy?"**

From what do living things get their energy?	For what do living things use the energy?
• producers get energy from sunlight	• life processes

Where do living things come from?

Use with textbook pages 14–21.

 Reading Check

1. What is the cell theory?

_____

_____

_____

_____

2. Why do scientists think viruses might be living things?

_____

_____

_____

_____

 *In Your Own Words*

Highlight the three main ideas of the cell theory. Put each idea in your own words.

 Check For Understanding

As you read about viruses, highlight the parts that help you understand what a virus is.

The Cell Theory

The invention of the microscope let scientists discover cells. Over a period of about 200 years, scientists studied cells in great detail. These studies helped scientists develop the *cell theory*. The *cell theory* is a set of three statements that explain what living things are made up of and where they come from.

◆ *Statement 1:* All living things are made up of one or more cells. This is one of the characteristics of living things. (Refer to page 8 in your textbook.)

◆ *Statement 2:* All new cells come from pre-existing cells. This is a different way of saying that living things reproduce—another characteristic of living things. (Refer to page 11 in your textbook.)

◆ *Statement 3:* The cell is the basic unit of life. This means that the cell is the most simple thing that has all the characteristics of living things. If a thing is missing even just one of those characteristics, it is not a cell.

Viruses—Living, Non-living, or Something Else?

A virus is a strand of genetic material encased in a protective coating of protein—a protein coat. A virus has just one of the characteristics of living things: It can reproduce. But, a virus cannot reproduce on its own. It must enter and take over a living cell so that it can reproduce.

Most scientists used to think that viruses are not living things. This view may be changing. The table outlines why.

Why Scientists' View of Viruses May Be Changing

What Scientists Have Learned Recently About Viruses	Comments
New, very large viruses are discovered.	These viruses have more genetic material than other known viruses. Some of it has never been seen before in viruses.
The new viruses and genetic material are studied and compared with known viruses.	Studies suggest that viruses might have been more like living cells long ago in Earth's ancient past. As time passed, viruses might have evolved to become the kinds of things they are today.

Cell Theory

Use with textbook pages 16–17.

1. Explain what the three parts of the **cell theory** mean.

   a) The cell is the basic unit of life.

   _____

   b) Cells come from pre-existing cells.

   _____

   c) All living things are made up of one or more cells.

   _____

2. Identify the part of the **cell theory** that explains each of the following statements. The table has been partially completed for you.

	Statement	Part of the Cell Theory
a)	A nerve cell by itself is alive.	The cell is the basic unit of life.
b)	An orca is a multicellular organism.	All living things are made up of one or more cells.
c)	A bacterium splits into two new daughter cells.	Cells come from pre-existing cells.
d)	New skin cells are produced through cell division.	
e)	*Paramecium* is a single-celled organism.	
f)	Diatoms are unicellular algae found in the ocean.	
g)	A fairy ring mushroom is composed of many cells.	
h)	A plant cell takes in carbon dioxide and releases oxygen.	
i)	A white blood cell engulfs a bacterium and then digests it.	
j)	Cells are often referred to as the building blocks of life.	
k)	A cell is the structural unit of life that can perform different life functions.	
l)	A bud grows off the yeast cell and eventually separates to form a new cell.	

Comparing a Cell to a Virus

Use with textbook pages 18–19.

1. Complete the Venn diagram to compare and contrast a cell with a virus. Part of the Venn diagram has been completed for you.

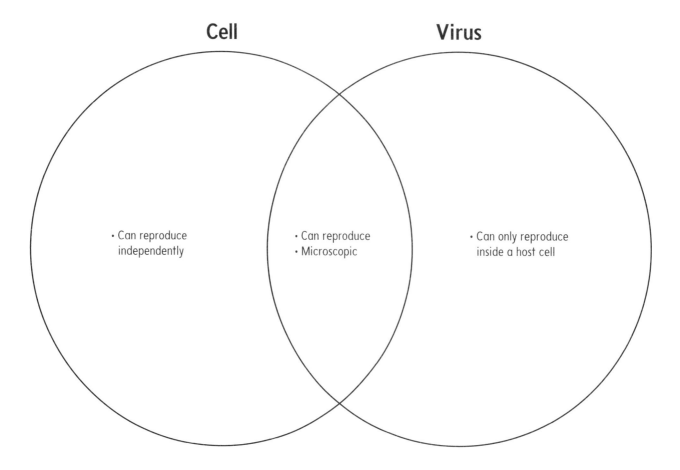

Are Viruses Alive?

Use with textbook pages 18-19.

1. Identify which of the following statements provide evidence that viruses are living things and which support that they are non-living particles.

	Statement	Living or Non-living?
a)	Viruses do not use energy.	
b)	A virus can evolve or change over time.	
c)	Viruses do not produce any waste products.	
d)	Viruses can exist in an inactive or dormant state.	
e)	A virus can reproduce only by infecting a host cell.	
f)	Many viruses have the same 400 protein folds as living cells.	
g)	A virus is a particle with genetic material surrounded by a protein coat.	
h)	A virus is dependent on a host cell's structures and processes to produce more viral particles.	
i)	Viruses have the ability to pass on their genetic information to future generations.	
j)	Viruses do not have the internal structures needed to produce more viruses on their own.	
k)	Viruses cannot take in nutrients like consumers or produce their own food like producers.	
l)	Viruses cannot carry out many life processes like digestion, respiration, and circulation.	
m)	There are no internal activities that occur inside a virus when it is not in contact with a host cell.	
n)	Some viruses, like the Mimivirus and the Megavirus, may have evolved from a common ancestor that was able to produce its own proteins.	

1.2 Assessment

Match each term on the left with the best description on the right. Each description may be used only once.

Term	Description
1. _____ host	A. inactive
2. _____ fibres	B. the cell that a virus infects
3. _____ viruses	C. has instructions to make new viruses
4. _____ dormant	D. particles that can cause colds and flus
5. _____ protein coat	E. outer layer that surrounds the genetic material
6. _____ genetic material	F. structures on a virus that help it attach onto a cell

Circle the letter of the best answer for questions 7 to 16.

7. The three statements of the cell theory

    A. explain how cells interact with other cells.

    B. are still not considered to be evidence by most scientists.

    C. are based on a collection of observations made of living cells.

    D. describe a series of hypotheses made from experiments involving living cells.

8. Which of the following is an example of the statement "all living things are made up of one or more cells"?

    A. A bacterium is a unicellular organism.

    B. A plant cell is the smallest living thing.

    C. A red blood cell carries oxygen around the body.

    D. A sea star has the ability to regenerate lost body parts.

9. A bud grows off the side of a Hydra and becomes an independent organism when it breaks off from the parent. Which part of the cell theory does this statement describe?

    A. A cell is the fundamental unit of life.

    B. New cells come from pre-existing cells.

    C. Living things are made up of one or more cell.

    D. This statement does not describe any part of the cell theory.

10. Scientists originally did not think viruses were alive because

    A. they looked different from a typical cell.

    B. they believed that viruses could not evolve.

    C. viruses were too microscopic for them to see.

    D. they did not have all the characteristics of living things.

11. Which of the following structures do all viruses have in common?

    A. a fatty coat

    B. cellular proteins

    C. genetic material

    D. a carbohydrate membrane

12. What does a virus depend on for reproducing more viruses?

    A. energy

    B. nutrients

    C. living cells

    D. other viruses

13. Why are viruses often referred to as parasites?

    A. They absorb nutrients from a host cell to survive.

    B. They live on the surface of a host cell to obtain energy.

    C. They have to infect and use a host cell's machinery in order to reproduce.

    D. They require the host cell to carry out their life processes like digestion and respiration.

14. What part of the virus is essential for taking over a host cell?

    A. tail

    B. protein coat

    C. lipid membrane

    D. genetic material

15. Which of the following characteristics do viruses share with living things?

    A. They can reproduce.

    B. They take in nutrients.

    C. They are made of cells.

    D. They produce waste products.

16. Which of the following statements is true of viruses?

    A. They can use energy from the nutrients that they take in.

    B. They reproduce in a host cell and have the ability to grow as they multiply in the host cell.

    C. They do not display any of the characteristics of living things except the ability to reproduce.

    D. They do not display any of the characteristics of living things, except the ability to produce waste products and respond to environmental stimuli.

17. Complete the following Frayer model diagram for viruses.

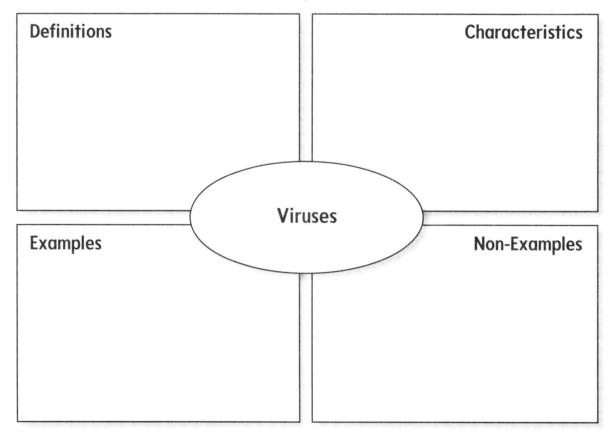

How are cells different from one another?

Use with textbook pages 24–33.

Two Types of Cells

There are two main types of cells. These are **prokaryotic cells** and **eukaryotic cells**.

Prokaryotic cells include bacteria. The genetic material of these cells is not enclosed by a membrane. Prokaryotic cells are smaller and simpler in structure than eukaryotic cells.

Eukaryotic cells make up living things that include plants and animals. The genetic material of the cells is enclosed by a membrane. The cells also have other structures called organelles that have specialized functions.

Comparing Plant and Animal Cells

Plant and animal cells have most of the same organelles. The chart below shows what plant and animal cells have in common and what they do not have in common. Some basic information about these organelles is found on page 29 of your textbook.

Plant Cells	Organelles	Animal Cells
✓ yes	cell membrane	✓ yes
✓ yes	cell wall	✗ no
✓ yes	chloroplasts	✗ no
✓ yes	cytoplasm	✓ yes
✓ yes	mitochondria	✓ yes
✓ yes	nucleus	✓ yes
✓ yes	vacuoles	✓ yes
✓ yes	vesicles	✓ yes

 Create a Quiz: Part I

After you read about plant and animal cells, create a five-question quiz based on what you have learned. Include your answers. Then trade your quiz with a classmate.

Reading Check

What are the key differences between plant and animal cells?

_____

_____

_____

_____

Create a Quiz: Part 2

After you read about photosynthesis and cellular respiration, create a new five-question quiz.

Reading Check

What are the key differences between photosynthesis and cellular respiration?

_____

_____

_____

_____

Comparing Photosynthesis and Cellular Respiration

The chloroplasts of plant cells let them make food for the plant through the process of photosynthesis. The mitochondria of plant cells and animal cells let them release energy from food to power their life functions.

The table below compares and summarizes these key processes.

	Photosynthesis	Cellular Respiration
What is it?	• A series of chemical changes green plants use to capture the Sun's light energy and transform it into chemical energy that is stored in energy-rich food substances such as sugars.	• A series of chemical changes that let living things release the energy stored in energy-rich food substances such as sugars to fuel all life functions.
Which living things use it?	• Only green plants and certain kinds of single-celled organisms.	• Nearly all living things.
How is energy changed?	• Light energy is changed to chemical energy.	• Chemical energy is changed to other forms of energy such as kinetic (motion) energy and heat.
What substances does it use?	• carbon dioxide • water	• glucose and other sugars • oxygen
What substances does it produce?	• glucose and other sugars • oxygen	• carbon dioxide • water
Why is it important?	• Photosynthesis transforms the Sun's energy into a form that living things can use to survive. • Photosynthesis produces the oxygen that most living things need to survive.	• Cellular respiration releases the stored chemical energy that living things use to survive. • Cellular respiration produces the carbon dioxide that green plants need to carry out photosynthesis.

Prokaryotic and Eukaryotic Cells

Use with textbook pages 26–29.

1. Complete the concept definition maps for a prokaryotic cell and a eukaryotic cell. Give the definition, characteristics, and examples for these two main types of cells.

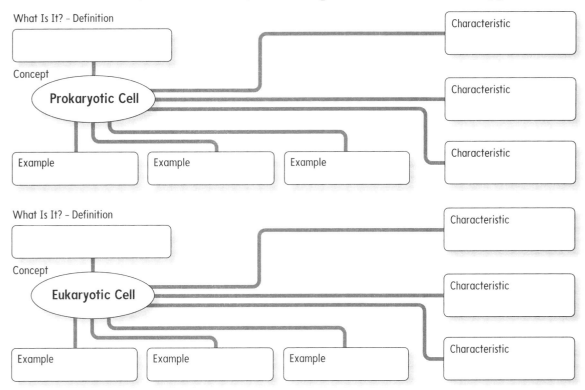

2. What key feature is used to classify cells into two categories: prokaryotic and eukaryotic? _____

3. Describe how prokaryotic cells are different from eukaryotic cells.

_____

4. A student looks at several slides under the microscope of four different cells. Classify these cells as prokaryotic or eukaryotic and explain what characteristic is used to place these cells into each group.

a) stem cell _____

b) heart cell _____

c) halophile (archaea that live in high salt environments)

_____

d) streptococcus (bacterium that causes strep throat)

_____

The Function of Cell Structures

Use with textbook page 29.

1. Cell structures have a specific role or function that supports the life processes of the cell. In your own words, describe the role of each cell structure and indicate which cell it is found in by circling the appropriate word.

Cell Membrane	Cell Wall	Nucleus
Function:	*Function:*	*Function:*
_____	_____	_____
_____	_____	_____
_____	_____	_____
_____	_____	_____
Found in which cells?	Found in which cells?	Found in which cells?
Plant Animal Both	*Plant Animal Both*	*Plant Animal Both*
Chloroplast		**Mitochondria**
Function:		*Function:*
_____		_____
_____		_____
_____		_____
		_____
Found in which cells?		Found in which cells?
Plant Animal Both		*Plant Animal Both*
Vesicles	**Vacuoles**	**Cytoplasm**
Function:	*Function:*	*Function:*
_____	_____	_____
_____	_____	_____
_____	_____	_____
_____	_____	_____
Found in which cells?	Found in which cells?	Found in which cells?
Plant Animal Both	*Plant Animal Both*	*Plant Animal Both*

2. List one cellular process that the cell would not be able to carry out if the following cell structures were unable to carry out their function:

   a) cell membrane _____

   b) nucleus _____

   c) mitochondria _____

   d) chloroplast _____

A Plant Cell Is Like a Shopping Mall

Use with textbook page 29.

A simile is a figure of speech that compares two things that are not alike by using the word "as" or "like." For example, she moved as quiet as a mouse; the water surface was smooth like glass.

1. Compare a cell to a shopping mall by filling in the blanks in the pictures below.

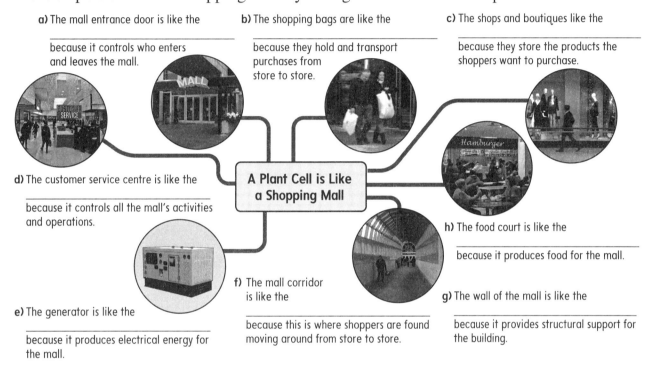

a) The mall entrance door is like the
_____
because it controls who enters
and leaves the mall.

b) The shopping bags are like the
_____
because they hold and transport
purchases from
store to store.

c) The shops and boutiques like the
_____
because they store the products the
shoppers want to purchase.

d) The customer service centre is like the
_____
because it controls all the mall's activities
and operations.

A Plant Cell is Like
a Shopping Mall

h) The food court is like the
_____
because it produces food for the mall.

e) The generator is like the
_____
because it produces electrical energy for
the mall.

f) The mall corridor
is like the
_____
because this is where shoppers are found
moving around from store to store.

g) The wall of the mall is like the
_____
because it provides structural support for
the building.

2. Compare a cell to a movie theatre. Complete the following table.

Cell Structure	Is Like	Because....
the cell membrane	the ticket booth	it controls who gets to see the movie by allowing only people with purchased tickets to enter the theatre

Rate of Photosynthesis

Use with textbook pages 30–31.

Photosynthesis is a process in which plants capture the Sun's light energy and convert carbon dioxide and water into sugar (food) and oxygen. A student wanted to conduct an experiment to determine the effect of light intensity on the rate of photosynthesis. The lab set-up is shown below.

Light from Lamp

Gas

Bubbles

Water and Baking Soda

Green Aquatic Plant

1. What could be a possible hypothesis for this experiment?

_____

_____

2. What could the student use as a control in the experiment? Why is this necessary?

_____

_____

3. What is the independent variable in this experiment?

_____

4. What is the dependent variable in this experiment?

_____

5. Why was baking soda added to the water?

_____

6. The student made some observations during the experiment and noticed that as she increased the light intensity, more bubbles formed. The student recorded the number of bubbles formed by the aquatic green plant. What do you think the bubbles represent?

_____

7. Using a data table, the student recorded the number of bubbles that formed and floated to the top of the water in the funnel. The student then plotted a graph, as shown below. The student decided that the rate of photosynthesis was going to be represented by the number of bubbles formed.

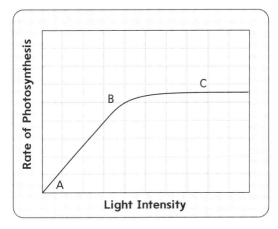

Analyze the graph shown above. Describe what each part of the graph represents.

a) Part A

_____

b) Part B

_____

c) Part C

_____

8. The student noticed that after a while the aquatic green plant did not produce as many bubbles as it did at the beginning, even when she increased the light intensity. What could the student do to get the plant to produce more bubbles?

_____

9. What could the student conclude from this experiment?

_____

1.3 Assessment

Match each cell structure on the left with the best function on the right. Each function may be used only once.

Cell Structure	Function
1. _____ vesicle	A. controls cell activities
2. _____ vacuole	B. stores food, waste, and water for the cell
3. _____ nucleus	C. provides protection and support for the cell
4. _____ cell wall	D. provides a jelly-like environment where organelles can float
5. _____ cytoplasm	E. regulates the movement of materials going into and out of the cell
6. _____ chloroplast	F. transports materials around the cell as well as in and out of the cell
7. _____ mitochondrion	G. converts food and oxygen into carbon dioxide, water, and energy for the cell
8. _____ cell membrane	H. converts light energy, carbon dioxide, and water into food for the cell and oxygen

Circle the letter of the best answer for questions 9 to 17.

9. Which of the following is an example of a prokaryotic cell?

   A. a root cell

   B. a flu virus

   C. a skin cell

   D. a bacterium

10. What is the key difference between a prokaryotic cell and a eukaryotic cell?

   A. the ability to move

   B. the need for oxygen to survive

   C. the ability to carry out photosynthesis

   D. the presence or absence of a nucleus

11. Which of the following statements describes what prokaryotic cells have in common with eukaryotic cells?

   A. They both are the same size.

   B. They both are membrane-bound organelles.

   C. They both carry out life processes needed to survive.

   D. They both have genetic material enclosed inside a nucleus.

12. A plant is given a substance that prevents the chlorophyll in the leaves from capturing light energy. Which of the following describes what is expected to happen to the plant?

  A. The plant will start to lose water.

  B. The plant will lose its rigid structure and start to wilt.

  C. The plant will not be able to produce chemical energy for cellular processes.

  D. The plant will not be able to produce carbon dioxide needed for cellular respiration to occur.

13. *Euglena* is a unicellular organism that is able to produce its own food because of the presence of many green organelles in its cytoplasm. Which of the following can you infer about *Euglena* based on the information given?

I	It is a prokaryotic cell.
II	It is a photosynthetic organism.
III	It has the green pigment chlorophyll.

  A. I and II only   **C.** II and III only

  B. I and III only   **D.** I, II, and III

14. Which of the following lists two cell structures found in plant cells but not animal cells?

  A. cell wall and chloroplasts

  B. vacuoles and chloroplasts

  C. mitochondria and cell wall

  D. nucleus and cell membrane

15. Which of the following correctly compares what processes occur in plant cells and animal cells?

	Animal Cells	Plant Cells
A.	Photosynthesis	Cellular respiration
B.	Cellular respiration	Cellular respiration
C.	Cellular respiration	Photosynthesis
D.	Cellular respiration	Cellular respiration and photosynthesis

16. Which of the following describes why photosynthesis and cellular respiration are complementary processes?

    A. One process stores food, the other releases food.

    B. One captures sunlight, the other releases sunlight.

    C. Both have to occur the same time in order for cells to store energy.

    D. The products of one process are necessary as reactants for the other process.

17. Which of the following explains why organisms can die if they do not get oxygen for their cells?

    A. The cells will not be able to move around to get food to survive.

    B. The cells in the organism will not be able to convert energy into food for the cell.

    C. There will be an imbalance of carbon dioxide compared to oxygen gas in the cell.

    D. Their cells will not be able to carry out cellular respiration to produce energy for essential life processes.

18. Complete a concept map for types of cells. The graphic organizer has been partially completed to help guide you.

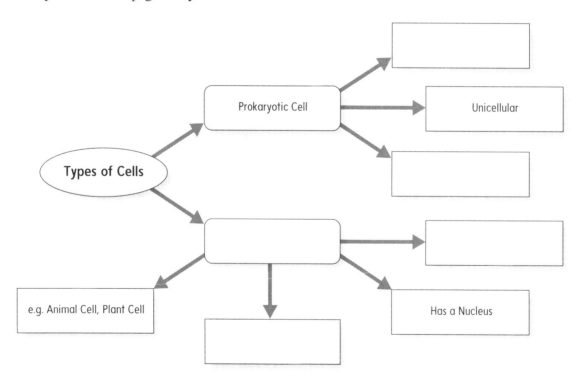

What interactions occur between humans and micro-organisms?

Use with textbook pages 38–45.

Micro-organisms

Micro-organisms, or microbes for short, are so small that a microscope is needed to see them. Bacteria are an example.

How Microbes Help Ecosystems

Some microbes are **producers**. They are the first links in the food chain for many kinds of living things. They also make oxygen.

Some microbes are **decomposers**. They return nutrients to the environment. Other living things use these nutrients for their life functions.

Some kinds of bacteria grow on the roots of plants such as peas and beans. These plants need nitrogen, and the microbes make it available to them in a form they can use.

Harmful and Helpful Interactions with Microbes

Some microbes hurt us (and other living things) by making us sick or causing illnesses that threaten life. Others help us by keeping us healthy or providing many of the products we eat or use each day.

Examples of Interactions with Microbes

Some Harmful Interactions	Some Helpful Interactions
• Pathogens are microbes that can make us sick. • Some microbes cause food to spoil. • Some microbes cause wood to rot.	• Some microbes help us digest food and prevent infection. • Microbes are used in food processing, drug, and agricultural industries. • Microbes are used in waste management.

 *Check for Understanding*

As you read this section, highlight the main point of each paragraph. Use a different colour to highlight an example that helps explain the main point, or write your own.

Reading Check

1. What is a microbe?

_____

_____

_____

_____

2. Give an example of how microbes can be helpful and another example of how microbes can be harmful.

_____

_____

_____

_____

How Small Are Microbes?

Use with textbook pages 40-41.

The following diagram shows the relative sizes of various microbes. For each microbe, determine how many would fit end-to-end along a straight line that measures 1 m in length. A sample calculation has been provided to guide you.

E. Coli (1000 nm x 3000 nm)

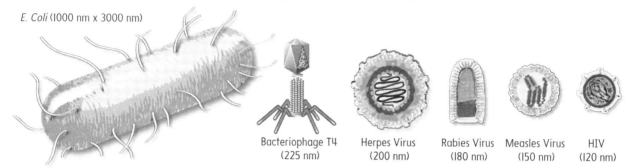

Bacteriophage T4 (225 nm) Herpes Virus (200 nm) Rabies Virus (180 nm) Measles Virus (150 nm) HIV (120 nm)

Note: metre is a base unit

prefix "nano" means 1 billionth

$$1 \text{ nm} = \frac{1}{1\ 000\ 000\ 000 \text{ m}}$$

$$= 0.000\ 000\ 001 \text{ m}$$

Sample Calculation:

How many *E. Coli*, with length of 3000 nm, would fit end-to-end on a straight line that measures 1 m in length?

Step 1: Convert nanometres to metres to calculate the actual length of the microbe in metres. Write the amount and unit given.

3000 nm

Step 2: Multiply by a fraction with the nanometre unit in the denominator and the metre unit in the numerator. There are 1 000 000 000 nm in 1 metre.

$$3000 \text{ nm} \times \frac{1 \text{ m}}{1\ 000\ 000\ 000 \text{ nm}}$$

Step 3: Cancel the common units in the numerator and the denominator.

$$3000 \text{ n\cancel{m}} \times \frac{1 \text{ m}}{1\ 000\ 000\ 000 \text{ \cancel{nm}}} = 0.000\ 003 \text{ m}$$

So, 3000 nm = 0.000 003 m.

Step 4: To determine how many microbes fit onto a 1 m line, divide 1 m by the actual length of the microbe in metres.

$$\frac{1 \text{ m}}{0.000\ 003 \text{ m}} = 333\ 333 \text{ } E. \text{ } Coli \text{ in 1 m}$$

Microbe	Length in nanometres (nm)	Calculations	Length in metres (m)	Number of microbes that would fit on a I m line
Bacteriophage (virus that attacks bacteria)	225 nm			
Herpes Virus (virus that causes cold sores)	200 nm			
Rabies Virus (virus that causes inflammation of the brain)	180 nm			
Measles Virus (virus that causes measles)	150 nm			
HIV (virus that causes AIDS)	120 nm			

Roles of Microbes

Use with textbook pages 40-43.

Complete the following crossword puzzle by using the clues and vocabulary list provided.

Vocabulary

chloroplast
decomposers
food
food poisoning
medicines
microbes
micro-organisms
nitrogen
nutrients
pathogens
photosynthesis
phytoplankton
toxins
water treatment
  plants

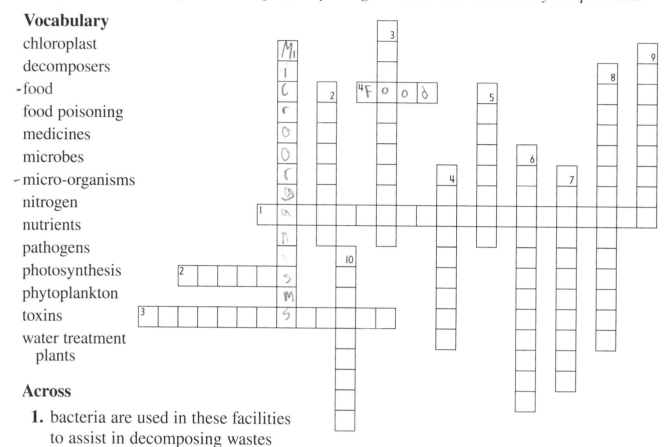

Across

1. bacteria are used in these facilities to assist in decomposing wastes
2. poisons
3. condition caused by *E. Coli, Listeria,* and *Botulism*
4. bacteria that make things like cheese, chocolate, and yogurt

Down

1. organisms that need a microscope to be seen
2. short form for micro-organism
3. bacteria that break down dead organisms to return nutrients to the soil
4. substance made available due to bacteria decomposing waste materials
5. nutrient made available to plants by bacteria in root nodules of peas and beans
6. microbes that live in oceans and lakes that produce 50% of the oxygen in the atmosphere
7. organelle found in producers that carry out photosynthesis
8. cellular process carried out by producers to make oxygen
9. organisms that cause diseases
10. examples include antibiotics and insulin made by bacteria

Useful Microbes

Use with textbook pages 42–43.

1. Complete the following concept map to illustrate the positive contributions that useful microbes make to the lives of humans.

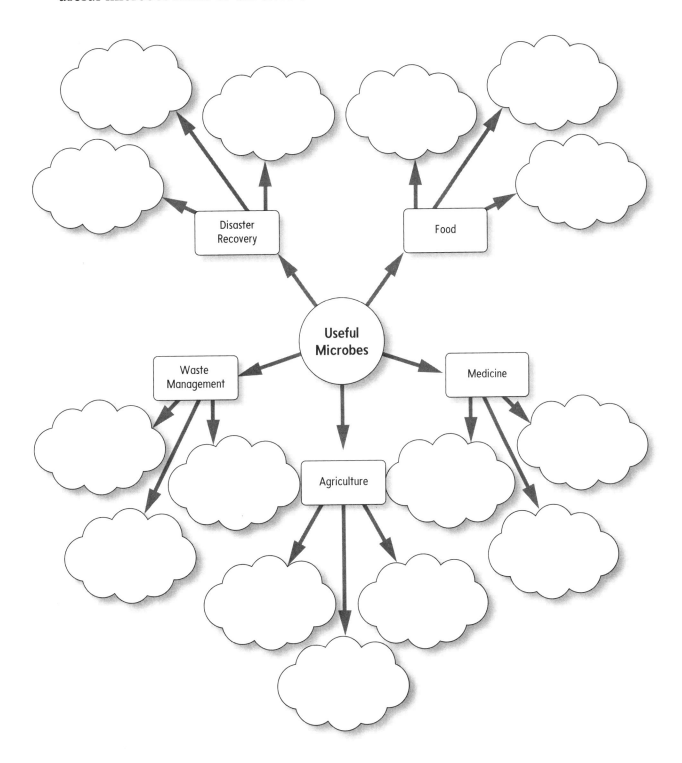

Pathogens That Cause Food Poisoning

Use with textbook pages 42-43.

Norovirus, Listeria, Salmonella, E. Coli, and *Campylobacter* are microbes responsible for causing food poisoning. In the last few decades, these microbes have been found in contaminated food. The average numbers of cases each year in Canada are shown in the following table.

Microbes	Food-borne Illnesses	Hospitalization
Norovirus	1 million	1 180
Listeria	178	150
Salmonella	88 000	925
E. Coli	12 800	245
Campylobacter	145 000	565
Total Cases	1 245 978	3 065

(Source: Government of Canada)

1. Create a pie chart from the hospitalization data given in the table. Show the data in the pie chart as percents.

2. Which microbe is the leading cause of food-borne illnesses and hospitalizations?

   _____

3. Which two bacteria have caused the greatest number of cases of food-borne illness?

   _____

4. What percent of hospitalizations are due to *Campylobacter?*

_____

5. Since *Salmonella, E. Coli, Listeria,* and *Campylobacter* have been linked to food poisoning, what are these four microbes also known as?

_____

6. According to the data, which one microbe results in 30% of the hospitalizations for food-borne illnesses.

_____

Use the following bar graph of Deaths Caused by Food-borne Illnesses to answer questions 7 to 9.

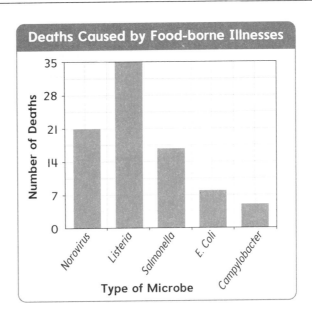

7. Which microbe is responsible for the greatest percent of deaths related to food-borne illnesses?

Listeria

8. Which microbe contributes to about 10% of the deaths related to food-borne illnesses?

E. Coli

9. What percent of food-borne illness related deaths are caused by Salmonella?

17

10. What precautions can people can take to prevent food-borne illnesses?

Checking their food before eating it.

1.4 Assessment

Match each term on the left with the best description on the right. Each description may be used only once.

Term	Description
1. _____ microbe	A. short form for micro-organism
2. _____ producer	B. organism that can cause a disease
3. _____ pathogen	C. an organism that requires a microscope to be seen
4. _____ decomposer	D. organism that breaks down dead and waste materials
5. _____ micro-organism	E. organism that can produce its own food through photosynthesis

Circle the letter of the best answer for questions 6 to 15.

6. Which of the following is not referred to as a micro-organism?

   A. ant on a log

   B. phytoplankton in the ocean

   C. yeast used to make beverages

   D. influenza virus that causes the seasonal flu

7. Where can microbes be found on the human body?

I	on the skin
II	in the airway
III	in the urogenital tract

   A. I and II only   **C.** II and III only

   B. I and III only   **D.** I, II, and III

8. Which of the following correctly matches the microbe with a possible location where it could be found?

	Type of Microbe	Possible Location
A.	archaea	root nodules of clover
B.	producer	at the bottom of the ocean on the sea floor
C.	decomposer	on a fallen tree that has been struck by lightning
D.	nitrogen fixer	inside the intestine of a human

9. Through genetic engineering, bacteria are used to do which of the following?

I	make drugs
II	attack and kill viruses
III	produce drought-resistant crops

  A. I and II only   **C.** II and III only

  B. I and III only   **D.** I, II, and III

10. Which of the following does not describe a pathogen?

  A. It is usually harmless.

  B. It can make people sick.

  C. It is a disease-causing agent.

  D. It can produce toxins or poisons.

11. Which of the following organisms are examples of pathogens?

  A. Bacteria in the intestine help digest food.

  B. Wood-decay fungus eats moist wood, which leads to the wood rotting.

  C. Bacteria produce erythromycin, an antibiotic used to treat infections.

  D. Bacteria in the mouth cause gum disease, resulting in inflammation of the gums.

12. Which of the following microbes are used to break down waste and pollutants in industrial sewage treatments?

  A. producers   **C.** decomposers

  B. pathogens   **D.** nitrogen fixers

13. Which of the following microbes could be called "extremists"?

  A. archaea   **C.** pathogens

  B. bacteria   **D.** decomposers

14. Which of the following are examples of the benefits of bacteria?

I	cause food to spoil
II	produce insulin for diabetic people
III	used to genetically modify tomatoes so they become frost tolerant

  A. I and II only   **C.** II and III only

  B. I and III only   **D.** I, II, and III

15. Which of the following statements explains why farmers alternate between growing corn for one year and then legumes the next year?

    A. Legumes help replenish the supply of usable nitrogen in the soil.

    B. Legumes can recycle nutrients, while corn cannot recycle nutrients.

    C. Legumes will help decompose the nutrients left behind by the corn for plants to use.

    D. Legumes balance things out by absorbing less oxygen, while the corn absorbs more oxygen from the atmosphere.

16. Micro-organisms play three important roles in the ecosystem: decomposers, nitrogen fixers and producers. Complete the following spider map/chart by providing a function, descriptions, and some examples of these different ecological roles. The chart has been partially completed to help guide you.

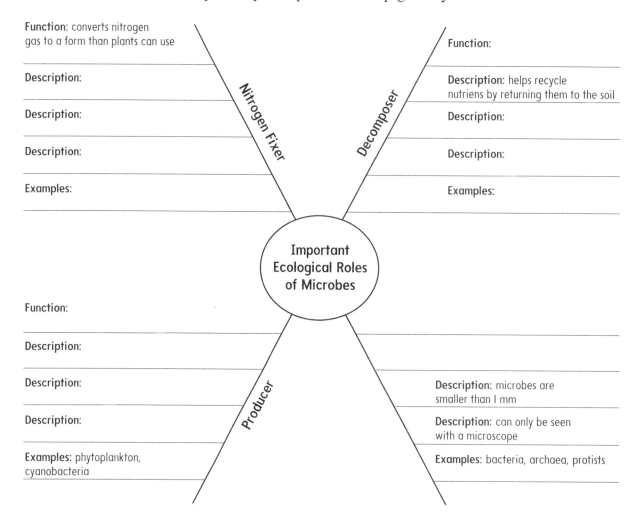

How does the body protect us from pathogens?

Use with textbook pages 46-55.

The Immune System Fights Pathogens and Infection

The immune system has three lines of defence against pathogens that cause disease and infection.

First Line: Body Structures and Secretions

- Body structures include skin and hairs and hair-like structures in your nose and throat.

- Secretions include mucus, sweat, and body acids.

Second Line: White Blood Cells and Inflammation

- White blood cells can surround and kill pathogens.

- Inflammation happens when an area is hurt or infected. The affected area gets red and swollen. White blood cells move in to kill pathogens and keep infection from spreading.

Third Line: Specialized White Blood Cells

- Specialized white blood cells recognize a pathogen after fighting it so they can respond quickly if the same pathogen invades the body again.

Types of Disease Occurrence

- An **epidemic** occurs when a disease affects more people in a certain area than would normally be expected.

- An **outbreak** is an epidemic in a limited area.

- A **pandemic** is an epidemic that spreads over many countries or the whole world.

Immunity and Impacts of Disease

Some people in a population have a natural ability to resist the pathogens that cause a disease. This is called immunity. Over time, immunity spreads through a population. As a result, fewer people die or get sick when a disease occurs.

Disease has social and economic impacts on society. When people are sick, or in cases of an outbreak, they may not be able to work or travel. Businesses lose money. Medical costs increase.

 Create an Outline

Make an outline of the information in this section. Use the headings, numbered points, and bulleted points to help you.

 Reading Check

1. Identify the three lines of defence against pathogens.

   ○ Body structures & Secretions. ○ White blood cells & inflammation. ○ Specialized white blood cells.

2. What is immunity and how does it develop in a population?

   Some people naturally have the ability to resist the pathogens. It over time spread throughout the population.

The First Line of Defence

Use with textbook page 48.

1. Give the function of the immune system.

The immune system is the defence against antigens.

2. In the diagram, identify three parts of the body that are part of the immune system's first line of defence. For each part of the body, provide a description, describe its structure, and give its function in the space provided.

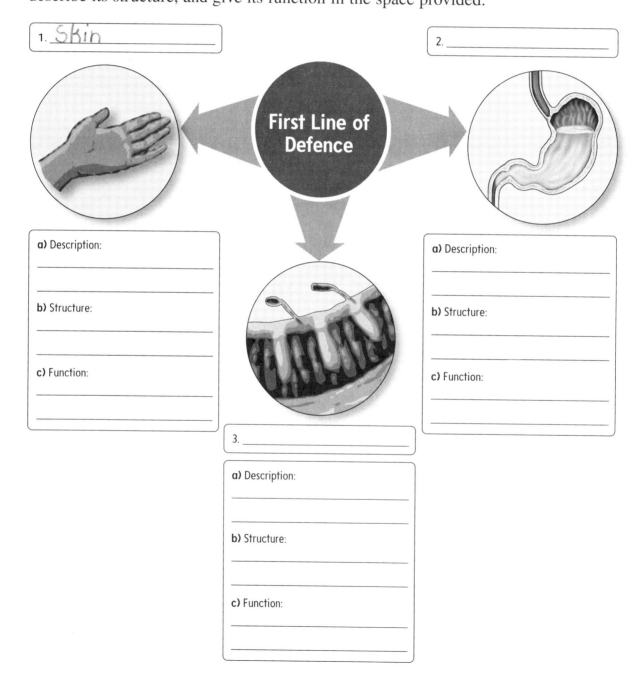

1. Skin

First Line of Defence

2. _____

a) Description: _____

b) Structure: _____

c) Function: _____

a) Description: _____

b) Structure: _____

c) Function: _____

3. _____

a) Description: _____

b) Structure: _____

c) Function: _____

The Body's Lines of Defence

Use with textbook pages 48-49.

In each of the following scenarios, indicate which of the human body's lines of defence (first, second, or third) would be responsible for defending it against pathogens.

1. A student touches a doorknob that has some viruses on it. Which line of defence will try to protect the student from the viruses on her hand?

   The acid on her skin.

2. A boy breathes in some air-borne viruses floating in the room. Which line of defence will try to protect the boy from the viruses that entered through his nose?

   The hairs which grow inside his nose.

3. A girl eats a piece of contaminated meat that has been left out for hours. Which line of defence will try to protect the girl from the *Salmonella* on the meat?

   The saliva in her mouth and acid in her stomache.

4. The hepatitis virus is attacking the liver cells and producing more viral particles in the body. Which line of defence will try to protect the individual from the hepatitis virus that is in the body?

   _____

5. A man has a large, deep wound in his leg because he was cut by a sharp piece of metal. The break in the skin on his leg starts to become red and swollen. Which line of defence will try to protect the man?

   _____

6. A woman has bronchitis. She is experiencing shortness of breath, and has a persistent cough and a high fever. Which line of defence will try to protect the woman from the pathogen that is making her sick?

   _____

7. A young boy accidentally steps on a rusty nail with his bare foot. He now has a puncture wound and his foot starts to become inflamed. Which line of defence will try to protect the boy from the bacteria that cause tetanus?

   _____

Flu Season

Use with textbook pages 50–52.

In the 2015–2016 flu season, there were over 33 000 cases of influenza, or the flu, reported to the Government of Canada Flu Watch. There were four main strains of the influenza virus during that season: three main types of Influenza A and one main type of Influenza B. Use the following data from the government of Canada for the 2015–2016 flu season to answer the following questions.

Data from 2015–2016 Flu Season (August 30, 2015–August 13, 2016)

Age	Cases of Influenza A	Cases of Influenza B	Total Cases of Influenza A and Influenza B
<5	4544	1774	6318
5-19	2414	2705	5119
20-44	5835	2208	8043
45-65	6428	1111	7539
65+	4896	1612	6508
Total Number	24 117	9410	33 527

(Source: Government of Canada)

1. Which age group had the greatest number of Influenza A cases?

   Age group with 45-65.

2. a) Which age group had the greatest number of Influenza B cases?

   Age group with 20-44.

   b) Based on this age range, what could you infer about where this group of individuals contracted the Influenza B virus?

   Most likey from work and or school.

   c) If this age group had to stay home due to illness for several weeks, how would school absenteeism impact these individuals academically?

   Their grades would go down hill and they would fail.

   d) How would the school absenteeism impact the parents or guardians of these individuals?

   The parents/guardians would recieve the illness.

3. Which age group had the most total cases of Influenza A and Influenza B?

   Age group 20-44.

4. Given that the total population of Canada in April 2015 was 35 749 600, what percentage of Canadians reported getting the flu?

   About 35 716 073 percent reported the flu.

5. Looking at the number of people in the main working groups (both age groups 20–44 and 45–65), what do you think the economic impact of the flu would have been on the working groups?

   _____

   _____

   _____

6. a) What percent of the total cases of Influenza A and Influenza B were in the age group 65+?

   _____

   b) Why would health officials consider the 65+ segment of the population to be at higher risk than others if they became ill with the flu?

   _____

   _____

   _____

7. Pose one question and answer it using the data shown in the table.

   _____

   _____

   _____

8. Write two questions that you could research from the data shown in the table.

   _____

   _____

   _____

Epidemic, Outbreak, and Pandemic

Use with textbook pages 50-52.

1. What two key factors distinguish an epidemic from an outbreak and a pandemic?

   _____

2. For each case described below, indicate whether it is an example of an epidemic, an outbreak, or a pandemic.

   a) In 1994, over 23 000 deaths occurred in refugee camps in the Congo due to cholera. _____

   b) In 2003, SARS killed over 800 people worldwide. _____

   c) In 2014, cholera spread rapidly to over 42 countries with 190 549 reported cases and 2231 deaths. _____

3. In each of the following scenarios, identify whether it has a social impact, an economic impact, or both on human populations.

   a) Thousands of deaths were reported during the H1N1 pandemic.

      _____

   b) There was a decline in tourism due to the spread of the Zika virus.

      _____

   c) There was a SARS outbreak and travel restrictions were issued to the affected countries. _____

   d) During the cold and flu season, there was an increase in absenteeism and lower productivity in the workplace. _____

   e) Diamond markets were closed during an Ebola outbreak because diamond miners refused to enter the mines, which were in the outbreak region.

      _____

   f) Borders were closed to beef and cattle products after cases of mad cow disease were detected. No beef product imports were permitted from the affected country. The infected cattle were then put down for precautionary measures.

      _____

1.5 Assessment

Match each term on the left with the best description on the right. Each description may be used only once.

Term	Description
1. ____ immunity	A. an individual's ability to fight pathogens
2. ____ inflammation	B. consists of white blood cells and inflammation
3. ____ immune system	C. process that causes an injured body part to become red and swollen
4. ____ first line of defence	D. consists of the skin, hair in the respiratory tract, and acid in the stomach
5. ____ second line of defence	E. body system that is responsible for defending the body against pathogens

Circle the letter of the best answer for questions 6 to 14.

6. Which of the following are considered to be the first line of defence?

I	tiny hairs in the throat
II	sweat on the forehead
III	mucus layer inside the nose

   A. I and II only

   B. I and III only

   C. II and III only

   D. I, II, and III

7. What is part of the second line of defence?

   A. skin

   B. viruses

   C. antibodies

   D. white blood cells

8. Which of the following describes when pathogens usually encounter the second line of defence?

   A. when the pathogens get past the first line of defence

   B. when the pathogens have defeated the third line of defence

   C. when the pathogens are killed by the strong acid in the stomach

   D. when the pathogens get trapped by the mucus in the throat and swallowed

9. Which of the following conditions are usually associated with an inflammation?

I	chills
II	redness
III	swelling

    A. I and II only

    B. I and III only

    C. II and III only

    D. I, II, and III

10. Which of the following scenarios is an example of an epidemic?

    A. 50 cases of meningitis in British Columbia

    B. a plague that kills 10 million people in the Americas, Africa, and Asia

    C. over 10 000 cases of SARS in multiple countries in Asia, Canada, and the USA

    D. thousands of cases of the Zika virus in several countries in South America, Central America, and Asia

11. HIV and AIDS have killed over 25 million people in several continents over the last three decades. This is an example of

    A. a pandemic.

    B. an outbreak.

    C. an epidemic.

    D. a natural resistance.

12. Which of the following are examples of economic impacts of an outbreak?

I	Farmers had to kill millions of livestock animals that were infected with the pathogen.
II	The cost for hospitalization and medical care was about $10 billion because of the outbreak.
III	There was a ban on the import of meat due to suspected cases of products contaminated with listeria.

    A. I and II only

    B. I and III only

    C. II and III only

    D. I, II, and III

13. If a person has natural immunity to the rabies virus, what does this mean?

    A. The person's immune system is compromised.

    B. The person has no immunity to the rabies virus.

    C. The person will die from the infection immediately.

    D. The person cannot get sick if he is infected with the rabies virus.

14. Which of the following could help scientists learn more about how to treat Ebola virus disease if they were to study individuals with a natural immunity to this disease?

    A. examining the first line of defence in these individuals

    B. investigating how these individuals contracted the virus

    C. seeing how severe the inflammation gets after the infection starts

    D. looking at the white blood cells in these individuals' immune system

15. Complete the Venn diagram to compare and contrast the first, second, and third lines of defence.

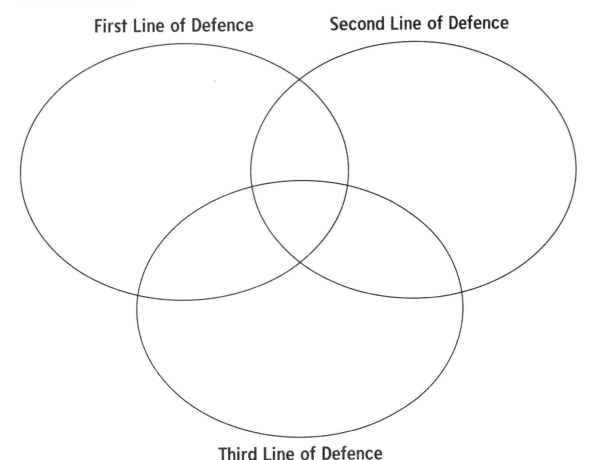

What medicines help protect us from microbes that make us sick?

Use with textbook pages 64-75.

 *Identify Definition*

As you read this section, highlight the definition of the two key terms that are described.

 *Reading Check*

1. What are two main sources for medicines?

_____

_____

_____

_____

2. How are vaccines different from antibiotics?

_____

_____

_____

_____

Medicines come from different sources. Traditional medicines of First Peoples come from resources in nature, such as plants. Other medicines such as vaccines and antibiotics are made by drug companies in laboratories.

Vaccines

A **vaccine** is a substance that helps provide immunity against a pathogen without causing illness. The vaccine can be part of a bacterium or virus. It can also be a weakened or inactive form of a pathogen.

Vaccines "teach" the immune system to recognize a pathogen. As a result, the immune system can react quickly if the real pathogen infects the body in future.

Getting a vaccine protects people against getting a disease, and it helps to stop the spread of disease. It also can prevent an outbreak from getting worse.

Antibiotics

An **antibiotic** fights infections caused by bacteria. It either kills the bacteria, or it prevents the bacteria from reproducing. Each antibiotic works against a specific type of bacteria. Antibiotics do not work on an infection caused by a virus.

Antibiotics are so good at treating illness that they have become overused. This can make antibiotics less effective as time passes. Some bacteria have developed a resistance to the antibiotics that are used to kill them.

Traditional Plant Medicines

Use with textbook pages 66–67.

1. Indian hellebore, devil's club, and Pacific yew are plants used by some First Peoples for medicinal purposes. How do you think traditional knowledge of these plants has been passed on from generation to generation?

   I think they have been passed down by stories on how they heal.

2. What major stakeholder do you think would benefit from the traditional knowledge and practices of First Peoples?

   Major stakeholders should learn and use the knowledge of the medical plants.

3. The conservation and management of using plants for medicinal purposes is a very important issue. List two things that you think should be considered when people harvest medicinal plants from the forests of B.C.?

   To make sure they arent dieased and to also make sure the plants get the dirt washed off so it dosent enter the wound and make it worse.

4. Overexploitation occurs when a natural resource is harvested to the point where it cannot be recovered. Do you think that there should be a system in place that records which plants are being collected for medicinal purposes, the location from which these plants are collected, and how much is harvested to prevent overexploitation? Explain your answer.

   Yes, if we don't then we may not have anymore of that plant left in forests.

5. What questions do you think major stakeholders should ask First Peoples if the stakeholders want to make use of First Peoples knowledge of medicinal plants?

   How do you use them? How do you know if its poisonous or diseased? Are there any wounds you shouldn't use them on? (etc......)

How Vaccines and Antibiotics Work

Use with textbook pages 68-71.

1. Compare and contrast how vaccines and antibiotics work by completing the different parts of the graphic organizer shown below.

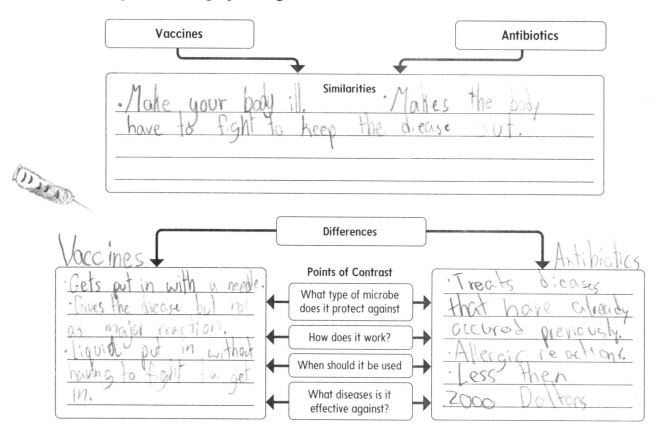

| Vaccines | Antibiotics |

Similarities

·Make your body ill. ·Makes the body have to fight to keep the diease out.

Differences

Vaccines

·Gets put in with a needle.
·Gives the diease but not as major reaction.
·Liquid put in without having to fight to get in.

Points of Contrast

- What type of microbe does it protect against
- How does it work?
- When should it be used
- What diseases is it effective against?

Antibiotics

·Treats dieases that have already occured previously.
·Allergic reactions.
·Less then 2000 Daltons

2. Create your own definition for:

   a) vaccine

   A fluid your diergnosed with by a needle.

   b) antibiotic

   A diease that fights to enter your body.

3. Your friend has a cold and thinks that she should see a doctor about getting a prescription for antibiotics. What would you say to your friend about using antibiotics to treat a cold?

   To let her nerves system fight it off so that she dosent recieve that same cold again.

Types of Vaccines

Use with textbook pages 68–69.

1. Four types of vaccines are administered to help prevent infections. Complete the following graphic organizer to show how these vaccines are different based on:

a) their components

b) the type of immune system response that they elicit

c) their description

d) the types of diseases that they are used to target

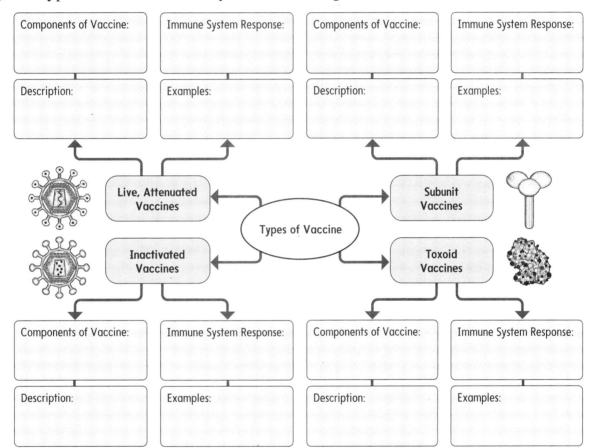

2. What do all four types of vaccines have in common?

   All vaccines diganose your immune system with a diease.

3. Explain why scientists have developed so many different types of vaccines, and not just one type, to prevent diseases?

   Its eaiser and theres less of a chance they do a miss mix.

How Effective are Vaccines?

Use with textbook pages 64–71.

Measles is a highly contagious disease caused by the measles virus. Measles symptoms include fever, runny nose, cough, sore throat, and a rash in the form of small red spots that appear all over the body. In a small percentage of people, if left untreated, measles can cause pneumonia, brain damage, deafness, and even death. Measles is usually spread when an infected person breathes, coughs, or sneezes. The virus can last up to two hours in a room after the person has left.

Before the measles vaccine was introduced in 1963, measles affected almost everyone. It would hit in two to three year cycles and would infect at least 350 000 people each year. Since the introduction of the vaccine, the rate of measles has dropped by over 99%.

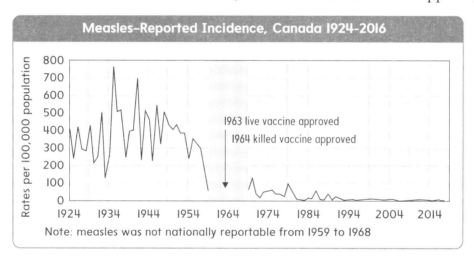

1. Looking at the pattern on the graph, what do you notice about the number of cases of measles since the introduction of the measles vaccine in 1963?

   Measles used to be outragous and when vaccines were created measles beame minor.

2. Based on the graph, how effective do you think the measles vaccine is at reducing infection? Explain why you think the vaccine is effective or not effective.

   Very affective because it decreasd majorly.

3. Do you think that measles is largely controlled in Canada by the use of the vaccine? Explain your answer.

   Yes because of the rate that it decreased at.

Use the following data to answer questions 4 to 8.

Number of Measles Cases Reported in B.C.

Year	2004	2005	2006	2007	2008	2009	2010	2011	2012	2013	2014
Number of Reported Cases	1	2	4	2	0	0	78*	10	2	17	343**

*2010 Data: A large outbreak occurred at the 2010 Winter Olympics in Vancouver and then spread throughout the province.

**2014 Data: About 343 confirmed measles cases were reported. This is the highest number since the introduction of the measles vaccine. Of the 343 reported cases, 325 were from a single community. Other areas in the province had 18 cases that year.

2014 Outbreak by Age

Age	Infant <1	1–4	5–19	20–59
Number of People Infected	5	17	280	41

4. a) During which two years were there no reported cases of measles?

2008 and 2009

b) What can you infer about the vaccination rates during these two years?

The vaccines worked really well but then failed during 2014

5. Which two years had the most reported cases of measles?

2010 and 2014

6. Why do you think there was an outbreak of measles at the 2010 Winter Olympics?

I think it might be because there was ALOT of people and it spread quickly and because of the tempture.

7. Look at the 2014 data. Which age group had the majority of the outbreak? Why do you think this is so?

5-19 has the most with 280 cases.

I think this age group because younger(ish) kids touch alot of stuff and older(ish) kids are around alot of other people at work and at high — school

1.6 Assessment

Match each term on the left with the best description on the right. Each description may be used only once.

Term	Description
1. _____ antibiotic	A. a substance that contains live microbes
2. _____ toxoid vaccine	B. a substance used to treat bacterial infections
3. _____ subunit vaccine	C. a substance that contains microbes that have been killed
4. _____ inactivated vaccine	D. a substance that contains only certain pieces of the microbe
5. _____ live, attenuated vaccine	E. a substance that contains toxins produced by certain types of bacteria

Circle the letter of the best answer for questions 6 to 13.

6. Which of the following factors put medicinal plants at greatest risk?

   A. red tide

   B. overharvesting

   C. toxoid vaccines

   D. antibiotic-resistant bacteria

7. Which of the following is important in the conservation of medicinal plants?

   A. selecting only plants native to B.C.

   B. ensuring that sustainable practices are in place

   C. harvesting plants that can eradicate viral diseases

   D. making sure that the plants are resistant to disease

8. What substances help the body build immunity by imitating a microbial infection?

   A. vaccines

   B. antibiotics

   C. medicinal clay

   D. medicinal plants

9. What vaccine is the closest thing to encountering a real pathogen?

A. toxoid vaccine

B. subunit vaccine

C. inactivated vaccine

D. live, attenuated vaccine

10. Which of the following is used to keep immunity levels up in a person?

A. antibiotics

B. booster shots

C. medicinal clay

D. medicinal plants

11. Health agencies strongly recommend that people get vaccines for which of the following reasons?

I	vaccines protect people from infections
II	vaccines can stop the spread of diseases
III	vaccines can help prevent an outbreak from becoming a pandemic

A. I and II only

B. I and III only

C. II and III only

D. I, II, and III

12. Which of the following describes how an antibiotic fights infections?

I	kills the microbe
II	prevents the microbe from growing
III	prevents the microbe from reproducing

A. I and II only

B. I and III only

C. II and III only

D. I, II, and III

13. When is a bacterium considered to be antibiotic-resistant?

   A. Antibiotics are not effective in killing this bacterium.

   B. The antibiotic will prevent the bacterium from entering the cell.

   C. The bacterium will die very quickly in the presence of antibiotics.

   D. The bacterium will reproduce quickly in the presence of antibiotics.

14. Complete the K-W-L chart shown below for antibiotics and antibiotic-resistant bacteria. In the K-column, fill in what you know. In the W-column, fill in what you want to know or wonder. In the L-column, fill in what you have learned.

K-W-L Chart Antibiotics and Antibiotic-Resistant Bacteria		
K – What I Know	W – What I Want to Know	L – What I Learned

What is the world's deadliest animal?

What's the Issue?

What do you think is the world's deadliest animal? Is it a lion? A crocodile? A shark? You might be surprised to learn that the mosquito is the deadliest animal. It kills more people than any other animal we come in contact with. How can such a tiny insect be so deadly?

When bitten by a female mosquito, a person comes into contact with the mosquito's bloodsucking mouthparts. The blood is not used for food by the mosquito. Instead, it is used as a source of protein for her eggs. A few days after the eggs receive the blood, the female lays the eggs in standing water or damp soil. About 48 hours later, approximately 200 new mosquito larvae hatch. Exact timing of the entire lifecycle of the mosquito depends on the species and environmental conditions.

Mosquitoes are found in over 100 countries and on every continent except Antarctica. There are over 2500 species of mosquito worldwide, and 82 species of them are in Canada. Mosquito-borne diseases cause over 725 000 deaths worldwide every year. The majority of these deaths are young children and the elderly in developing countries.

Species of Mosquito	Mosquito-Borne Diseases						
	Malaria	Dengue	Zika	West Nile Virus	Encephalitis (different strains)	Yellow Fever	Chikungunya
Anopheles	✔						
Culex				✔	✔		
Aedes		✔	✔			✔	✔

How do mosquitoes transmit disease?

In the last few years, with advances in microscopy, scientists have been able to learn more about how mosquitoes transmit disease. When a female mosquito bites, she sticks her proboscis (the pointy part of her mouth) into the person's skin. While the proboscis looks like one tiny spear, it is actually made up of six tiny needles, wrapped in a protective cover.

What do these needles do?

◆ Two of the needles have tiny teeth and saw through your skin.

◆ Two of the needles hold skin tissue apart.

◆ One of the needles inserts mosquito saliva that has an anti-coagulant in it, which causes the blood to flow more easily.

◆ One of the needles is used like a straw to suck up the blood.

During the biting process, some of the mosquito's saliva remains behind. This saliva may contain bacteria, viruses, or parasites that originate from the previous person who was bitten by the mosquito. Mosquitoes are the world's deadliest organism to humans because they are carriers of these lethal pathogens.

Neat Fact #1

Mosquitoes get their food from nectar and plants, not blood from biting humans!

Neat Fact #2

A mosquito can drink up to three times its weight in blood.

Neat Fact #3

Mosquitoes find humans from the exhalation of carbon dioxide.

Neat Fact #4

The red bump people get from a mosquito bite is a tiny allergic reaction to the mosquito saliva!

Dig Deeper

Collaborate with your classmates to explore one or more of these questions—or generate your own questions to explore.

1. What types of mosquitoes are found in your area of B.C.? Are they known to carry any diseases?

2. Where do most of the deadly mosquito-borne diseases occur on Earth? Are there similar climate conditions in these affected areas? What contributes to the growth and spread of mosquito-borne diseases?

3. What are some of the conditions that mosquitoes need to survive? What can you do around your home to prevent mosquitoes from breeding?

4. When is mosquito season in B.C.? What are some precautionary measures that you can take to help protect yourself against mosquitoes when you are outdoors during mosquito season?

5. Do some research on one of the mosquito-borne diseases. When was it discovered? Who is at risk? How many people are affected by this disease? What are some symptoms of this disease? In what part of the world does this disease usually occur? What are the treatments for this disease? Are there any vaccines available to help prevent this disease?

6. What are some health management strategies available to combat mosquito-borne diseases?

7. Suppose you are planning a trip to one of the countries that has mosquito-borne diseases. Find out what health precautions you should take before going to that country. Are there any medications or vaccinations that you can have before going to reduce the risk of infection?

8. What is the immune system response to one of these mosquito-borne diseases?

9. Has there been any epidemic, outbreak, or pandemic caused by mosquito-borne diseases in B.C.? In Canada? If so, how was it dealt with? What were some of the social and economic implications of this?

How does matter affect your life?

Use with textbook pages 94–103.

 *Create a Quiz*

After you read this page, create a five-question quiz based on what you have learned. Trade your quiz with a partner, and answer the questions.

The word "chemical" refers to anything that is matter. In the home, many chemical products have symbols on them to tell you about their safety. These are **Hazardous Household Products Symbols (HHPS)**.

The Borders

 Dangerous Container
The border that looks like a traffic yield sign means that the container is dangerous.

 Dangerous Product
The border that looks like a traffic stop sign means that the contents of the container are dangerous.

The Hazards

 Explosive
This symbol means that the container can explode. If it is punctured or heated, pieces can cause serious injuries, especially to the eyes.

 Corrosive
This symbol means that the product inside the container will burn the throat or stomach if swallowed and will burn skin or eyes on contact.

 Flammable
This symbol means that the product will catch on fire easily if it is near sparks, flames, or even heat.

 Poisonous
This symbol means that the product will cause illness or death if you eat or drink it. For some products, just smelling or licking them is enough to cause serious harm.

In school and in the workplace, chemical products have a different set of safety symbols on them. These symbols are part of the **Workplace Hazardous Materials Information System (WHMIS)**.

Exploding bomb (for explosion or reactivity hazards)	**Flame** (for fire hazards)	**Flame over circle** (for oxidizing hazards)
Gas cylinder (for gases under pressure)	**Corrosion** (for corrosive damage to metals, as well as skin and eyes)	**Skull and Crossbones** (can cause death or toxicity with short exposure to small amounts)
Health hazard (may cause or is suspected of causing serious health effects)	**Exclamation mark** (may cause less serious health effects or damage the ozone layer)	**Biohazardous** infectious materials (for organisms or toxins that can cause disease in people or animals)

You must work and act safely in your school laboratory. You must know the safety information in your textbook on pages xiv to xvii and pages 100 to 101. Your teacher may give you additional safety information.

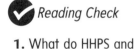 *Reading Check*

1. What do HHPS and WHMIS stand for?

_____

_____

_____

_____

2. How do the HHPS and WHMIS systems differ?

_____

_____

_____

_____

Identifying Hazardous Household Products Symbols (HHPS)

Use with textbook page 97.

1. What is the hazard associated with the following HHPS borders?

a) _____

b) _____

2. Complete the following table.

	HHPS Symbol	Degree and Type of Hazard	Safety Precautions Needed	Type of Product This Symbol Is Found On
a)		• caution (least severe) • explosive • can cause serious injuries if heated or punctured		
b)			• store away from heat and flames • use in a well-ventilated area	
c)				• toilet bowl cleaner • oven cleaner
d)			• do not make contact with skin • do not get in eyes • do not eat or drink • do not breathe in fumes • wear gloves • wear protective goggles and clothes • wash hands after using	

Understanding WHMIS and HHPS

Use with textbook pages 97 and 99.

1. You are about to use the following three household products. Identify the HHPS symbols found on each container and the hazards illustrated by these symbols. Describe the precautions you would take when using these products.

Household Item	Name of the HHPS Symbol	Hazard	Safety Precautions
Propane Gas			
Stain Remover			
Fondue Fuel			

2. Nitrous oxide gas (aka laughing gas), used in dental offices for sedation, is stored in containers under pressure and is highly flammable.

   a) What two WHMIS symbols would be on a safety label for nitrous oxide gas?

   _____

   b) What are the hazards associated with these WHMIS symbols?

   _____

   c) Describe two safety precautions you should take when using this gas.

   _____

   _____

   d) Suggest a place where this gas can be safely stored.

   _____

Safety Do's and Don'ts

Use with textbook pages 100–101.

Each of the following situations could happen in a science lab. Describe the unsafe practices and explain the safe and correct way to carry out the procedure.

1. You and your partner came to class late and missed the instructions on how to do the lab. You convince your partner that it is okay to start the lab without the teacher.

   Unsafe practice: _____

   Safe lab practice: _____

2. You are cold and decide to keep your long dangly scarf around your neck as you use the Bunsen burner.

   Unsafe practice: _____

   Safe lab practice: _____

3. You did not have time to eat lunch so you decide that you can eat your sandwich and drink your soda while you dissect the eyeball.

   Unsafe practice: _____

   Safe lab practice: _____

4. You just washed your hands but there are no paper towels available. You decide that it is okay to unplug your microscope by pulling on the cord.

   Unsafe practice: _____

   Safe lab practice: _____

5. While you are heating the solution in the test tube, you point it away from you but toward your partner.

   Unsafe practice: _____

   Safe lab practice: _____

6. You are asked to describe the odour of the solution in the beaker. You hold the beaker up close to your face and smell the fumes.

   Unsafe practice: _____

   Safe lab practice: _____

2.1 Assessment

Match each description on the left with the best HHPS symbol on the right. Each HHPS may be used only once.

Description	HHPS Symbol	
1. ____ Explosive	A.	D.
2. ____ Corrosive		
3. ____ Poisonous	B.	E.
4. ____ Flammable		
5. ____ Dangerous Contents	C.	F.
6. ____ Dangerous Container		

Match each description on the left with the best WHMIS symbol on the right. Each WHMIS symbol may be used only once.

Description	WHMIS Symbol	
7. ____ for fire hazards	G.	L.
8. ____ for oxidizing hazards		
9. ____ for explosion hazards	H.	M.
10. ____ may cause serious health effects		
11. ____ for compressed gas under pressure	I.	N.
12. ____ may cause less serious health effects		
13. ____ for organisms that can cause diseases	J.	O.
14. ____ for corrosive damage to metals, skin and eyes		
15. ____ may cause death or toxicity with exposure to small amounts	K.	

Circle the letter of the best answer for questions 16 to 26.

16. A hairspray can has a HHPS explosive symbol on it. Which of the following is a hazard associated with this product?

    A. It can explode.

    B. It can cause death if eaten.

    C. It can burn the throat if swallowed.

    D. It can easily catch fire near sparks.

17. Which of the following HHPS symbols would be found on a bleach bottle that has a chemical that can burn your skin on contact?

    A. corrosive

    B. explosive

    C. poisonous

    D. flammable

18. What WHMIS symbol would you expect to be on the label for a tank of helium gas that is used to fill balloons?

    A. gas cylinder

    B. flame over circle

    C. exclamation mark

    D. skull and crossbones

19. Sulfuric acid is known to cause severe burns on contact and cause death with exposure to small amounts. Which two WHMIS symbols would illustrate these hazards?

    A. corrosion and skull and crossbones

    B. flame over circle and exclamation mark

    C. skull and crossbones and health hazards

    D. flame and biohazardous infectious materials

20. After giving you an immunization shot, the nurse takes the needle and disposes of it in a yellow container. What WHMIS symbol would you expect to be on the container?

    A. health hazard

    B. exclamation mark

    C. skull and crossbones

    D. biohazardous infectious materials

21. You read the procedures to the lab, but you do not understand what to do with the four chemicals. What should you do next?

    A. Sit and wait until your partner helps you out.

    B. Ask your teacher for clarification before proceeding.

    C. Mix all four chemicals together hoping that there will be a reaction.

    D. Look over at the next table and copy what the other students are doing.

22. Which of the following is unsafe in the science classroom?

   A. wafting the fume toward your nose

   B. using a broken test tube to heat water

   C. wearing safety glasses while mixing chemicals

   D. disposing of chemicals in clearly marked containers

23. A student accidentally splashes some chemicals into his eyes during a lab. Which of the following is the best procedure to deal with this situation?

   A. Wash his face with soap and water.

   B. Try to remove the chemicals by rubbing his eyes.

   C. Dry his eyes with some paper towel until the chemicals are gone.

   D. Wash his eyes out immediately with water for 15 minutes at the eye wash station.

24. Which of the following are things a student should do before using a Bunsen burner with open flames?

I	Tie long hair back.
II	Put on safety glasses.
III	Remove dangling bracelets and necklaces.

   A. I and II only

   B. I and III only

   C. II and III only

   D. I, II, and III

25. Which of the following describes why it is important to make sure that your hands are dry when plugging an electrical device into a socket?

   A. to prevent burns

   B. to prevent electrocution

   C. to reduce the risk of fire

   D. to not damage the socket

26. Which of the following is the correct procedure to use while heating substances in glassware?

I	Use a test tube holder, not your hands, to pick up the test tube.
II	Set the heated test tube aside in a test tube rack to cool.
III	Point the test tube away from you but toward your partner while heating.

   A. I and II only

   B. I and III only

   C. II and III only

   D. I, II, and III

27. Complete a spider chart/map for safety rules in the science classroom. The graphic organizer has been partially completed to help guide you.

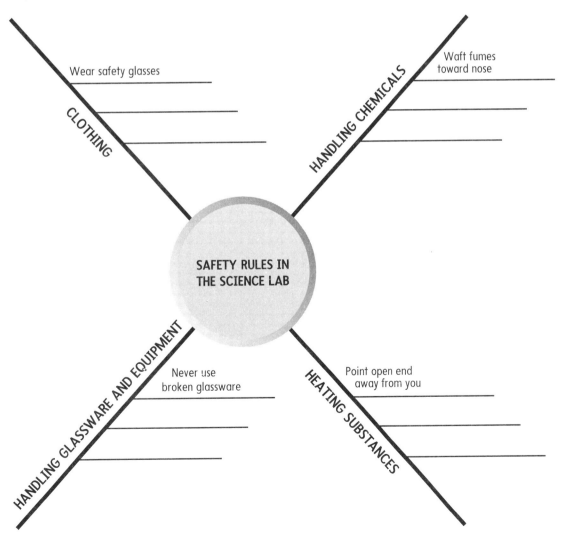

What are some ways to describe matter?

Use with textbook pages 110–125.

 *Summarize*

As you read this section, highlight the main point in each paragraph. Then, write a short paragraph to summarize what you have learned.

✓ *Reading Check*

1. How are physical changes different from chemical changes?

_____

_____

_____

_____

2. How is density related to the mass and volume of a substance?

_____

_____

_____

_____

Physical Changes and Properties

During a **physical change**, matter may change in its shape or appearance, but it keeps its identity (the type of matter it is) and its properties. **Physical properties** of matter are features that you can observe and measure without changing its identity.

If you can describe matter using measurements and numbers, the properties are **quantitative**. Examples are melting point, boiling point, and density. All other properties are **qualitative**. Examples are texture, smell, colour, and state.

Mass, Volume, and Density

Mass is the amount or quantity of matter in a sample. Mass is often measured in grams (g), kilograms (kg), and milligrams (mg).

Volume is the amount of space that a sample of matter takes up. The volume of solids is often measured in cubic metres (m^3) and cubic centimetres (cm^3). The volume of liquids and gases is often measured in litres (L) and millilitres (mL).

Density is the amount of mass in a given volume. Density is often measured in g/mL or g/cm^3. If you know the mass and volume of an object or substance, you can determine its density with this formula:

$$\text{Density} = \frac{\text{mass}}{\text{volume}}$$

$$D = \frac{m}{V}$$

Water has a density of 1 g/mL. Objects that have a density less than this will float on water. Objects that have a density greater than this will sink in water.

Chemical Changes and Properties

During a **chemical change**, one type of matter is changed to produce one or more different kinds of matter. The matter that is produced has a different identity and different properties from the original matter.

Chemical properties are features that describe the ability of matter to take part in a chemical change. Examples are the ability to burn (combustibility) and reactivity with acids.

The Law of Conservation of Mass

A scientific law describes a regular pattern that has been observed over a long period of time. For example, the **law of conservation of mass** is a scientific law that describes what happens in a chemical reaction to the reactants (the substances that react together) and the products (the substances that result from the reaction). The law of conservation of mass states that the mass of the products is always equal to the mass of the reactants.

Classifying Matter

All matter can be classified into two main groups: mixtures and pure substances.

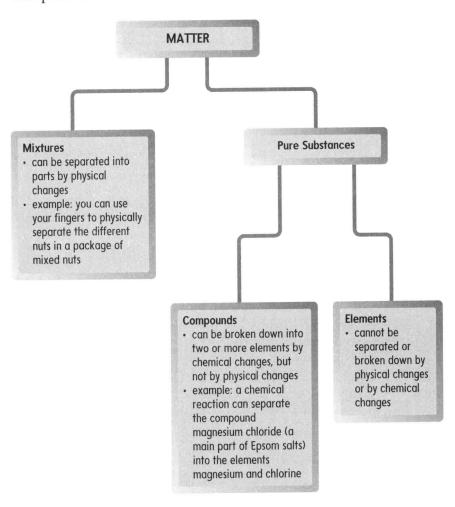

Creating a Density Tower

Use with textbook pages 114–115.

1. If the six substances listed below were poured into a beaker, where would they settle based on their densities? Draw a density tower and label the layers in the beaker.

Substance	Density (g/mL)
water	1.00
honey	1.42
baby oil	0.83
dish soap	1.03
maple syrup	1.37
vegetable oil	0.92

2. You are going to drop each of the following three objects into the beaker. In your density tower, draw and label where the objects will settle.

   cork: density = 0.24 g/cm^3

   marble: density = 2.5 g/cm^3

   plastic bead: density = 0.737 g/cm^3

3. Why do the substances not mix together, but instead form distinct layers? Explain.

   _____

4. How do the substances layer in a specific order from top to bottom?

   _____

5. What determines whether an object sinks or floats?

   _____

6. Is density affected by the amount of the substance? For example, what would happen if you added twice the amount (volume) of the least dense substance to the density tower? Would it still remain on top or sink lower?

   _____

   _____

7. An object has a density that is greater than the density of water. How could you make it float? Explain by giving a real-life example.

   _____

Density of Different Objects

Use with textbook pages 114–115.

Use the mass versus volume graph
to answer questions 1 to 4.

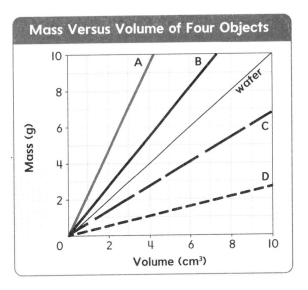

Mass Versus Volume of Four Objects

1. **a)** What is the mass of the four objects when the volume is 3 cm³?

    i. Object A = _____

    ii. Object B = _____

    iii. Object C = _____

    iv. Object D = _____

   b) What is the mass of water with a volume of 3 cm³? _____

2. **a)** Compare the masses of the four objects to the mass of an equal volume of
      water. Which objects are lighter than water and which are heavier than water?

   _____

   b) Predict which objects will float and which will sink in water.

   _____

3. Which object has the greatest density? Which object has the least density?

   _____

4. Water (1.0 g/mL), castor oil (0.956 g/mL), and corn syrup (1.38 g/mL) are poured
   into a graduated cylinder. Objects A, B, C, and D from above are then added to the
   liquids. List the order in which the three liquids and four objects would appear in
   the graduated cylinder from top to bottom.

   _____

Identifying Substances Based on Physical Properties

Use with textbook pages 112–113.

You are given two beakers, each with 200 g of a white crystalline powder. You are told one is sugar (sucrose) and the other is table salt (sodium chloride). The crystalline powders are not labelled. Design a test to determine which substance is salt and which substance is sugar, based on physical properties such as density and solubility. Prepare a step-by-step procedure to explain how this test might be done. Which variable(s) would you keep the same in your test? Which variables would you change?

1. List some qualitative physical properties that can be used to distinguish the two substances.

_____

Density

2. Suggest a testable question to investigate.

_____

3. How would you design an experiment to compare the density of table salt and sugar?

_____

_____

4. List the variables you would need to control.

_____

5. Other than tasting the white powders, explain how you would determine which beaker contains table salt and which one contains sugar. Note: Table salt has a density of **2.16 g/cm³** and sugar has a density of **1.59 g/cm³**. You may find completing the following table helpful.

Beaker A	Beaker B
Volume =	Volume =
Mass = 200 g	Mass = 200 g
Density =	Density =
Substance = ?	Substance = ?

_____

_____

Solubility

6. Suggest a testable question to investigate.

_____

7. How would you design an experiment to compare the solubility of table salt and sugar?

_____

_____

8. What are some variables that should be kept the same?

_____

Use the solubility graph to answer questions 9 to 11.

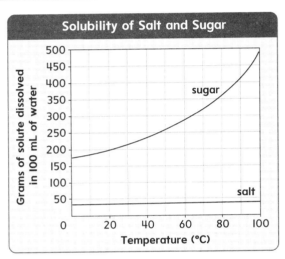

9. What does the graph show about the ability for sugar to dissolve in cold and hot water?

_____

10. Describe the ability of salt to dissolve in cold and hot water.

_____

11. According to the graph, what is the relative amount of sugar and salt that dissolves in 100 mL of water at 80°C? What does this suggest about the effect of temperature on the relative solubility of these two substances?

_____

12. Give two examples from everyday situations where you would find it useful to identify unknown substances. Explain how you would identify these substances.

_____

_____

Physical and Chemical Changes

Use with textbook pages II2–II3 and II8–I2I.

a) fireworks exploding   **b)** clothes drying

c) digesting hot dog

e) chopping wood

f) roasting marshmallows   **d)** turning on flashlight

1. Indicate whether each description represents a physical or a chemical change in the camping scenario shown above.

   a) fireworks exploding _____

   b) clothes drying _____

   c) digesting hot dog _____

   d) turning on flashlight _____

   e) chopping wood _____

   f) roasting marshmallows _____

2. Indicate whether the statement describes a physical or chemical property. Then, indicate the type of property.

	Statement	Physical or Chemical Property	Type of Property
a)	Wood is combustible.	chemical property	combustibility
b)	Aluminum tent poles are malleable.		
c)	Oxygen is a gas at room temperature.		
d)	The melting point of chocolate is 30°C.		
e)	Potassium in fireworks is very reactive.		
f)	Propane gas in the lantern is flammable.		

Mixture or Pure Substance?

Use with textbook page 124.

1. Complete the flowchart of matter. Use the following terms: **compounds, elements, mixture, pure substances**.

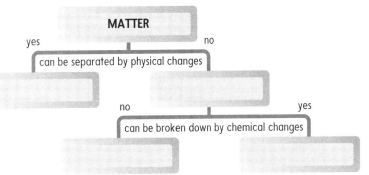

2. Complete the Venn diagram to compare and contrast a mixture with a pure substance.

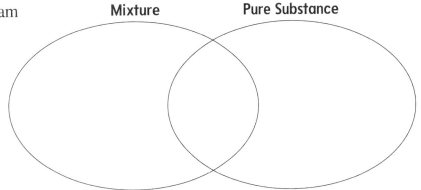

3. Indicate whether each sample is a mixture or a pure substance. If it is a mixture, list two substances that are part of the mixture.

	Sample	Mixture or Pure Substance?	Substances in Mixture
a)	air		
b)	iron		
c)	milk		
d)	water		
e)	blood		
f)	sugar		
g)	helium		
h)	concrete		
i)	hydrogen		
j)	sea water		
k)	lemonade		
l)	cake batter		
m)	granola bar		
n)	Italian salad dressing		

2.2 Assessment

Match each term on the left with the best description on the right. Each description may be used only once.

Term	Description
1. ____ lustre	A. ability to dissolve
2. ____ viscosity	B. ability to catch fire and burn
3. ____ solubility	C. soft shine that a surface has
4. ____ reactivity	D. rate at which a substance flows
5. ____ malleability	E. ability to be shaped by hammering
6. ____ melting point	F. ability to chemically react with another substance
7. ____ boiling point	G. temperature at which a substance changes from a liquid to a gas
8. ____ combustibility	H. temperature at which a substance changes from a solid to a liquid

Circle the letter of the best answer for questions 9 to 23.

9. Platinum is usually used to make wedding rings because it is soft, shiny, and easy to shape. Which of the following are the physical properties described?

   A. colour, viscosity, and ductility

   B. density, tarnish, and solubility

   C. texture, lustre, and malleability

   D. hardness, reactivity, and conductivity

10. Which of the following describes a quantitative physical property?

   A. Sulfur has a yellow colour.

   B. Mercury is liquid at room temperature.

   C. Sewer gas usually has a rotten egg smell.

   D. Ketchup is 50 000 times as viscous as water.

11. Which of the following describes the chemical property of a substance?

   A. The side of the car is starting to rust.

   B. The butter melts on top of the muffin.

   C. The paper is shredded into small pieces.

   D. Oil does not mix well with water because it is insoluble in water.

Use the table to answer questions 12 to 14.

Type of Wood	Density (g/cm³)
Cedar	0.55
Ebony	1.3
Maple	0.6
Spruce	0.45
Dogwood	0.75

12. Water has a density of 1 g/mL. Which types of wood listed in the table will float on top of water?

A. spruce and ebony

B. ebony and maple

C. cedar, maple, spruce, and dogwood

D. cedar, ebony, maple, spruce, and dogwood

13. If a cutting board has a mass of 1800 g and a volume of 3000 cm³, what type of wood is the cutting board made from?

A. cedar

B. ebony

C. maple

D. spruce

14. A rock with a volume of 10 cm³ and a density of 2.65 g/cm³ is placed in water. A piece of dogwood with a volume of 30 cm³ is also placed in the water. Predict what will happen to the rock and the piece of dogwood.

A. They will both sink.

B. They will both float.

C. The rock will float and the dogwood will sink.

D. The rock will sink and the dogwood will float.

Use the following diagrams to answer questions 15 to 17.

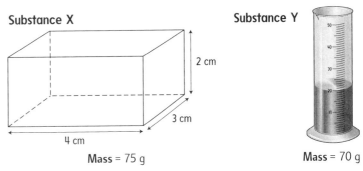

Substance X

2 cm

3 cm

4 cm

Mass = 75 g

Substance Y

Mass = 70 g

15. The volume of Substance X is greater than the volume of Substance Y.

A. The statement is true.

B. The statement is false.

C. There is not enough information to determine the volume of the two substances.

16. Which of the following compares the density of Substance X and Substance Y?

A. Substance X is denser than Substance Y.

B. Substance Y is denser than Substance X.

C. Both substances have the same density.

17. If Substance Y is placed in a beaker of water, what will happen?

A. Substance Y will mix with the water and form one layer.

B. Substance Y will float in water and form a layer above the water.

C. Substance Y will sink in water and form a layer below the water.

18. The mass of a metal ring is 116 g. You fill a graduated cylinder with 15 mL of water and drop the ring into the cylinder. The water level rises to the 26 mL mark. Which of the following could be the composition of the object?

	Metal Composition	Density (g/cm³)
A.	Silver	10.5
B.	Rhodium	12.41
C.	Gold	19.32
D.	Platinum	21.5

19. Which of the following is an example of a chemical change?

I	The bread starts to rise in the oven.
II	The egg white starts to turn into an opaque solid on the frying pan.
III	Steam from the shower starts to condense on the bathroom mirror.

A. I and II only   **C.** II and III only

B. I and III only   **D.** I, II, and III

20. Which of the following is an example of a physical change?

A. The silver ring is starting to tarnish.

B. The antacid helps calm your stomach.

C. A clump of clay is moulded into a bowl.

D. Milk goes sour when it is left out for days.

21. According to the law of conservation of mass,

    A. the mass of the reactants is equal to the mass of the products.

    B. the mass of the reactants is less than the mass of the products.

    C. the mass of the reactants is greater than the mass of the products.

    D. the sum of the mass of the reactants and products is equal to zero.

22. Which of the following are examples of mixtures?

I	a jar of nuts and bolts
II	trail mix consisting of a variety of nuts and dried fruits
III	carbon monoxide gas coming out of a car's exhaust pipe

    A. I and II only   **C.** II and III only

    B. I and III only   **D.** I, II, and III

23. Which of the following lists contains only individual elements?

    A. water, sugar, and salt

    B. carbon, copper, and iron

    C. tomato juice, propane, and soda pop

    D. sulfuric acid, magnesium, and chocolate chip cookies

24. Complete the following Frayer model diagram for chemical changes.

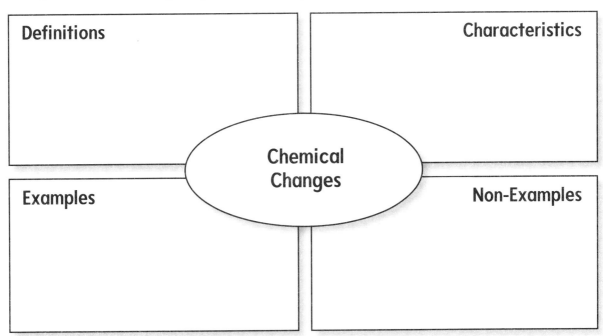

How can we describe and explain the states of matter?

Use with textbook pages 132–145.

 Identify Details

Use a highlighter to mark all the details about how the kinetic molecular theory explains matter and the ways it behaves.

The Kinetic Molecular Theory

The **kinetic molecular theory** explains what happens to the three states of matter as they undergo physical changes. According to the theory, all matter is made up of tiny particles. The particles are always moving, have space between them, and are attracted to one another. The table shows how the theory explains some observations about matter.

Observation	How the Kinetic Molecular Theory Explains It
There are three states of matter: solid, liquid, and gas.	• The particles of a solid move very slowly and are spaced very closely together. • The particles of a liquid move slowly (but faster than those of a solid) and are spaced a bit farther apart than those of a solid. • The particles of a gas move very quickly and are spaced very far apart.
The volume of matter changes when energy is added to it or removed from it. Adding energy to matter causes its volume to increase—it expands. Removing energy from matter causes its volume to decrease—it contracts.	• Adding energy to matter (such as heating it) speeds up the motion of its particles. They collide with each other more often, and they push each other farther apart. As a result, matter expands. • Removing energy from matter (such as cooling it) slows down the motion of its particles. They come closer together. As a result, matter contracts.
Adding or removing energy can cause matter to change its state.	Adding energy to matter makes its particles move faster: • Changing from solid to liquid: The extra motion causes the force of attraction between particles of a solid to get weaker, which lets them slide past each other. As a result, the solid is melting and eventually becomes a liquid. • Changing from liquid to gas: As particles move even faster, the force of attraction between gets even weaker, which lets them spread farther and farther apart. As a result, the liquid is boiling (or evaporating or vaporizing) and eventually becomes a gas. Removing energy from matter makes its particles move more slowly: • Changing from a gas to a liquid: This is condensing and is the reverse of what happens during boiling. • Changing from a liquid to a solid: This is freezing (or solidifying) and is the reverse of what happens during melting.
Solids such as salt and tea diffuse throughout liquids such as water.	• Particles of liquids move faster than particles of solid. The faster-moving liquid particles collide with the slower-moving solid particles, pushing them out of their position in the solid. At the same time, the solid particles fit into the spaces between the liquid particles. As a result, the solid spreads throughout the liquid.
Gas particles such as those from cooking food and cologne diffuse into gases such as air.	• Particles of different gases are spaced very far apart and move very quickly. As a result, the different gases mix together easily.

Visualizing the Kinetic Molecular Theory

Use with textbook pages 134, 135, and 138.

1. The key points of the kinetic molecular theory of matter are:

   a) All matter is made up of very small _____.

   b) There are a lot of empty _____ between the particles.

   c) Particles are always in constant random _____.

   d) Particles move because they have _____. As they gain energy, they move faster.

2. Windsurfers depend on the properties of the three states of matter to enjoy their water activity. They ride the waves of the water to perform jumps and spinning manoeuvres on their board. Their movement is powered by wind on the sail. In the diagram below, describe the particle spacing and movement in a solid, a liquid, and a gas. Indicate the relative amount of kinetic energy in each state of matter.

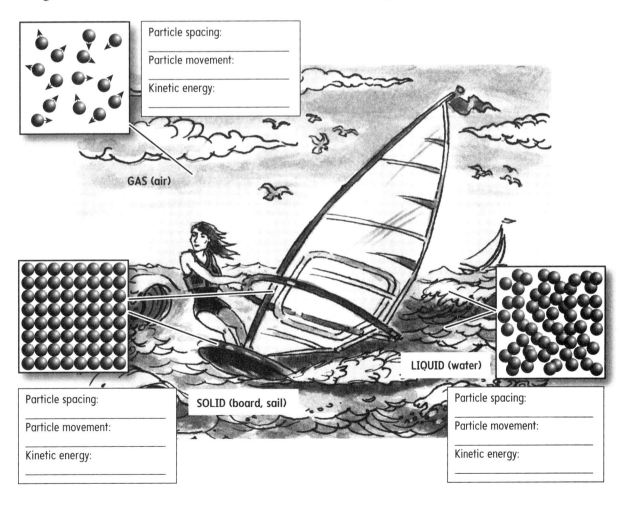

Particle spacing:
_____
Particle movement:
_____
Kinetic energy:
_____

GAS (air)

Particle spacing:
_____
Particle movement:
_____
Kinetic energy:
_____

SOLID (board, sail)

LIQUID (water)

Particle spacing:
_____
Particle movement:
_____
Kinetic energy:
_____

Properties of the States of Matter

Use with textbook pages 134, 135, and 138.

1. Complete the following table for solids, liquids, and gases. The table has been partially completed to help you with the descriptions.

	Solid	Liquid	Gas
Shape			• not fixed • takes the shape of the container
Volume		• fixed volume	
Mass			• definite
Arrangement of Particles		• randomly arranged • particles are touching, but able to move past one another	
Movement of Particles			• can move freely and quickly in all directions in the container

2. The metal lid on a jar of jam is screwed on tight. Use what you know about the behaviour of particles to explain whether it would be a good idea to run some cold or hot water under the lid to help to remove it.

_____

_____

3. Engineers recommend the use of structural steel columns and reinforced concrete slabs to build parking garages. The steel increases the strength of the concrete. These two materials are often used together because they have similar rates of thermal expansion. Use your knowledge of the kinetic molecular theory and thermal expansion to explain the importance of steel and concrete having almost the same expansion rates.

_____

_____

Changes of State

Use with textbook pages 139–141.

1. Label the diagram shown below using the following terms: **condensation, deposition, vaporization, melting, freezing,** and **sublimation**. Place the terms in the correct locations on the numbered arrows.

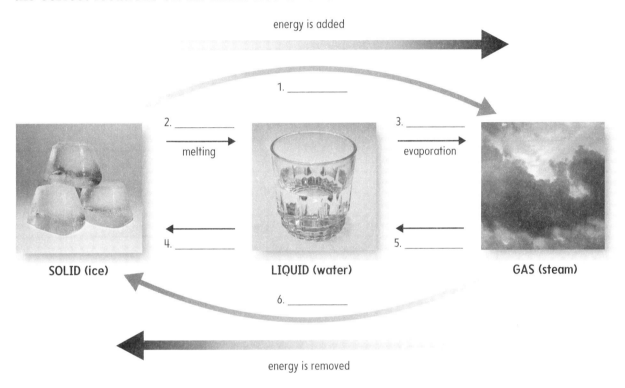

energy is added

1. _____

2. _____   melting   3. _____   evaporation

4. _____   5. _____

6. _____

SOLID (ice)   LIQUID (water)   GAS (steam)

energy is removed

2. Complete the following table by indicating the initial and final states of matter and whether kinetic energy is added or removed. Give an example of each of the changes of state.

State Change	State of Matter		Kinetic Energy		Example
	Initial State	Final State	Added	Removed	
Melting	Solid	Liquid			
Freezing					
Deposition					
Sublimation					
Vaporization					
Condensation	Gas	Liquid			Water droplets form on a bathroom mirror after a hot shower.

Changes of State of Silver

Use with textbook pages 139-141.

The graph shows how temperature changes as energy is added to silver.

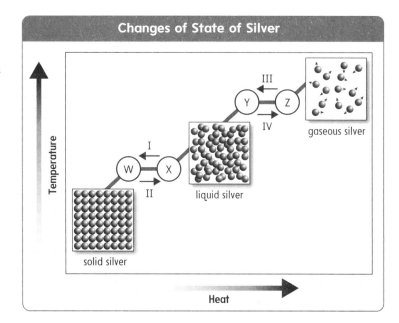

Changes of State of Silver

gaseous silver

liquid silver

solid silver

Temperature

Heat

1. What do points I, II, III, and IV on the graph represent?

   _____

2. Use the kinetic molecular theory to explain how liquid silver becomes solid silver.

   _____

3. What change of state occurs at points I, II, III, and IV on the graph?

   _____

4. What must be added to solid silver to cause it to change to a liquid?

   _____

5. What is happening to the particles during the process represented by IV on the graph?

   _____

6. If the temperature is increased, describe what happens to the kinetic energy of the particles in solid silver and the arrangement and movement of these particles. How is this change in motion detected?

   _____

7. Explain what the temperature from point W to point X on the graph represents.

   _____

8. Explain what the temperature from point Y to point Z on the graph represents.

   _____

9. Why is the temperature constant from point W to point X? What do you think is happening to the particles of silver as energy continues to be added to the silver?

   _____

Effects of Temperature on Diffusion

Use with textbook pages 134, 135, 138, and 143.

Three beakers and some tea bags are placed on a table. The first beaker has cold water, the second has hot boiling water, and the third has room temperature water.

1. Design a test to determine whether the temperature of water affects the rate of diffusion. Prepare a step-by-step procedure to explain how this investigation might be done.

   _____

   _____

   _____

   _____

2. List some testable questions to investigate.

   _____

   _____

3. Which variables would you keep the same in your investigation?

   _____

   _____

4. Which variable would you change?

   _____

5. What is the purpose of using the room temperature water?

   _____

6. Reflect on your experiences with diffusion. What new questions do you have about diffusion in everyday life? Come up with two questions about diffusion. State them in the form of testable questions.

   _____

7. State a hypothesis and a prediction based on your testable questions so that they can be answered through scientific investigation.

   _____

   _____

2.3 Assessment

*Match each description on the left with the state of matter on the right. Each state of matter may be used **more than once**.*

Description	State of Matter
1. _____ can diffuse the fastest	
2. _____ particles can only vibrate	
3. _____ has fixed shape and volume	
4. _____ moves quickly in all different directions	
5. _____ has shape and volume similar to plasma	
6. _____ state of matter that is the end result of melting	X Y Z
7. _____ particles are arranged in regular, repeating patterns	
8. _____ particles slip and slide past each other in a container	

Circle the letter of the best answer for questions 9 to 23.

9. Which of the following analogies are appropriate to explain the different states of matter?

I	Solid—people standing side by side in a crowded elevator
II	Liquid—people dancing and moving around other people in a gym
III	Gas—two people at opposite corners of an empty football stadium

   A. I and II only   **C.** II and III only

   B. I and III only   **D.** I, II, and III

10. Which state of matter is a gas-like mixture of positively and negatively charged particles that occur in the Sun and in lightning?

   A. gas   **C.** liquid

   B. solid   **D.** plasma

11. Which of the following has a definite volume, but its shape is determined by its surrounding?

   A. coffee   **C.** a helium balloon

   B. an apple   **D.** neon gas in an OPEN sign

12. What does the kinetic molecular theory explain?

    A. how particles behave when "their spacing and movement change"

    B. how to measure the kinetic energy of solids, liquids, and gases

    C. how to find the rate of diffusion of solids, liquids, and gases

    D. how to determine the change in temperature as a solid changes to a liquid and then to a gas

13. Which of the following are the key concepts of the kinetic molecular theory?

I	particles are in constant motion
II	matter is made up of very small particles
III	heat and kinetic energy make the particles move

    A. I and II only   **C.** II and III only

    B. I and III only   **D.** I, II, and III

14. What happens to a substance when energy is removed from it?

    A. The particles increase in volume.

    B. The particles become less dense.

    C. The particles take up more space.

    D. The particles move around at a slower rate.

15. Which of the following explains why running through air is easier than running through water?

    A. There are more empty spaces in air than water.

    B. The particles are more compact in air than water.

    C. Air is denser than water and easier to manoeuvre around.

    D. There are no particles in air, while there are lots of particles in water.

16. Which of the following changes of state involve energy being released to the environment?

I	deposition
II	vaporization
III	condensation

    A. I and II only

    B. I and III only

    C. II and III only

    D. I, II, and III

17. Which of the following describe melting?

I	energy is added
II	the opposite of freezing
III	change of state from a solid to a liquid

    A. I and II only

    B. I and III only

    C. II and III only

    D. I, II, and III

Use the diagram to answer questions 18 to 21.

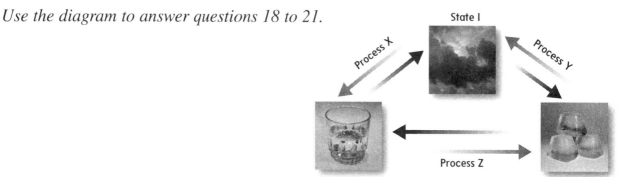

State I

Process X

Process Y

Process Z

State II

State III

18. Which of the following shows the three states of matter in order of increasing kinetic energy?

Least amount of kinetic energy	⟶	Greatest amount of kinetic energy
A	State I	State II	State III
B	State II	State I	State III
C	State III	State I	State II
D	State III	State II	State I

19. What represents **Process Y** in the diagram?

    A. melting

    B. freezing

    C. sublimation

    D. vaporization

20. Which of the following occurs during **Process Z**?

    A. Kinetic energy is added.

    B. Particles start to slow down.

    C. The volume becomes indefinite.

    D. Particles spread farther apart.

21. Which of the following is an example of **Process X**?

    A. the hardening of cement

    B. dew forming on grass in the morning

    C. liquid hand sanitizer evaporating from your hand

    D. the heat from the flame melting the wax on a birthday candle

22. Which of the following refers to the temperature at which a liquid becomes a gas?

    A. dew point

    B. boiling point

    C. melting point

    D. freezing point

23. When a metal expands due to a temperature increase, this is referred to as

    A. plasma

    B. thermal expansion

    C. a chemical change

    D. thermal contraction

24. Complete the Venn diagram to compare and contrast a solid, a liquid, and a gas.

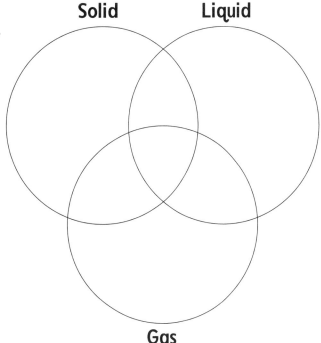

25. Create a mind map for matter. You may use lines to connect any two terms together. Use the following terms in your mind map:

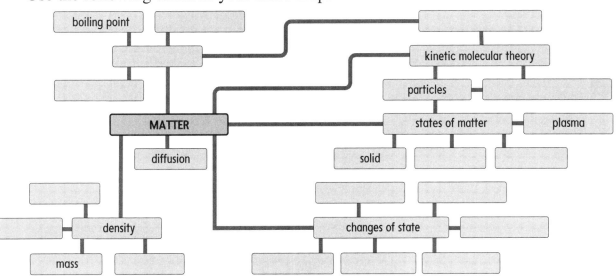

How can we investigate and explain the composition of atoms?

Use with textbook pages 152–167.

 *Check for Understanding*

As you read the section, re-read any parts you do not understand. Highlight any sentences that help you understand better. Put question marks beside any sentences that you still need help to understand.

Atoms

An atom is the smallest particle of an element that still has the properties of the element. Atoms are made up of smaller, subatomic particles. These are protons, neutrons, and electrons.

- Protons have a positive charge.

- Neutrons have no charge.

- Electrons have a negative charge.

Protons and neutrons form the nucleus of an atom, which is its positively charged central core. Electrons occupy the space that surrounds the nucleus.

Atomic Theory and Its Associated Atomic Models

In science, a theory provides a way to explain what something is or how it works or behaves. A model may be used to help illustrate certain key aspects of a theory. John Dalton proposed the first scientific theory for the atom. Here are the key points of his atomic theory.

- All matter is made of small particles called atoms.

- Atoms cannot be created, destroyed, or divided by chemical changes.

- All atoms of the same element have the same size, mass, and chemical properties.

- Atoms of a given element are different from the atoms of a different element.

- Compounds form when atoms of different elements link together in certain ways.

The model of the atom that Dalton used was a small, solid sphere such as a billiard ball. The chart shows how Dalton's model of the atom changed over the years.

Model of the Atom	Evidence for the Model
John Dalton's billiard ball model — hydrogen atom, oxygen atom	Dalton used the idea of atoms to explain the results of experiments that he did with compounds such as water and carbon dioxide.
JJ Thomson's plum pudding/ blueberry muffin model — electrons, positively charged atom	Thomson observed streams of negatively charged particles while studying electric currents in gas discharge tubes. He inferred that all atoms have these particles.
Ernest Rutherford's nuclear model — electrons move through empty space around the nucleus, nucleus made of positively charged protons and neutral neutrons	Rutherford exposed thin gold foil to streams of positively charged particles called alpha particles. Most of these particles pass through the foil. A small number of them were deflected as if they had struck something solid. Rutherford inferred that this "something solid" was the nucleus.
Niels Bohr's revised nuclear model — electrons, nucleus, energy levels or shells	Bohr made hydrogen gas glow by passing an electric current through it. He studied the light given off as electrons gain and give off energy. He proposed that electrons can only exist in specific energy levels around the nucleus.

The Model of the Atom Is Still Changing

Scientists have been able to show that the subatomic particles of atoms are themselves made up of even smaller particles.

- Protons and neutrons are made up of elementary particles called quarks that are bound together by other elementary particles called gluons.

- Electrons belong to a group of elementary particles called leptons.

- Research into the nature and composition of atoms is still ongoing.

_____

_____

_____

_____

✔ *Reading Check*

1. Identify the three main subatomic particles and where they are found in an atom.

   _____

   _____

   _____

   _____

2. How does the atomic theory differ from an atomic model?

   _____

   _____

   _____

Atomic Theory Timeline

Use with textbook pages 154–161.

Complete the following atomic theory timeline by filling in the blanks.

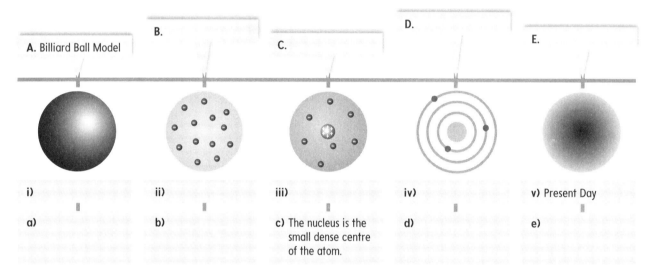

A. Billiard Ball Model   B.   C.   D.   E.

i)   ii)   iii)   iv)   v) Present Day

a)   b)   c) The nucleus is the small dense centre of the atom.   d)   e)

1. In the first row, label the illustrated atoms shown with the associated atomic model name. Choose from the following list:

   Blueberry Muffin Model, Bohr Model, Cloud of Electrons Model, Rutherford Model

2. In the second row, identify the individual associated with each proposed model of the atom shown in the diagrams. Choose from the following list:

   Bohr, Dalton, Rutherford, Thomson

3. In the third row, match the descriptions with the associated atomic model. Choose from the following list:

   • An atom is indivisible and indestructible.

   • Electrons occupy specific energy levels.

   • The atom has a spread-out cloud of negative charge.

   • An atom contains negatively charged particles called electrons.

4. Make a sketch to show how the model of the atom has changed since the model proposed by Bohr.

Rutherford's Gold Foil Experiment

Use with textbook pages 157–161.

Rutherford exposed a sheet of gold foil to a stream of positively charged alpha particles. The gold foil was surrounded by a detector, which lit up when the alpha particles hit the screen. Most of the alpha particles went through the gold foil, but some bounced backward from the foil. This experiment led to the discovery of the nucleus.

1. What do you think Rutherford's testable question was for the gold foil experiment that he designed?

_____

Use the following diagram to answer questions 2 to 5.

electrons scattered throughout

positive charge spread evenly throughout

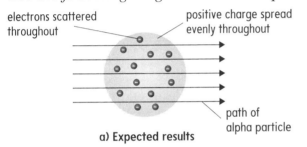

path of alpha particle

a) Expected results

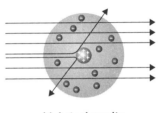

b) Actual results

2. What did Rutherford expect from his experiment, according to Thomson's model of the atom?

_____

3. List some observations from Rutherford's experiment and your interpretation of these observations.

	Observations	Interpretations
a)		
b)		
c)		

4. Would the observations be the same if Rutherford used a thin sheet of aluminum foil instead of gold foil? Why or why not?

_____

5. If Thomson's blueberry muffin model of the atom was correct, how would this have affected the results on Rutherford's gold foil experiment?

_____

Parts of an Atom

Use with textbook pages 162–163.

1. Define the following terms:

   a) atom _____

   b) subatomic particles _____

2. Use the following terms to label the parts of an atom: **electron, energy level, neutron, nucleus, proton**.

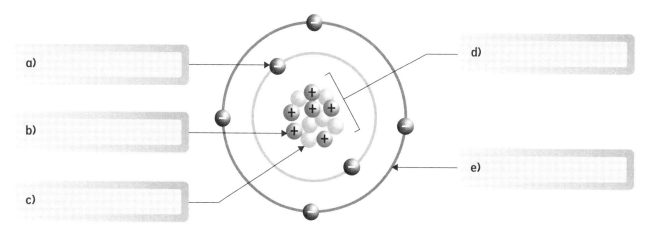

a)

b)

c)

d)

e)

3. Complete the following table describing the three subatomic particles.

	Proton	Electron	Neutron
Symbol			
Electric Charge			
Location in the Atom			

Quarks and Leptons

Use with textbook pages 164–165.

1. Matter is composed of _____ and _____ .
Quarks and leptons are examples of _____ .
There are six _____ of quarks. Both protons and neutrons are
known as _____ and are made up of three
quarks.

2. Label the following diagram showing the particles of matter. Choose from the
following list of terms: **electron, neutron, proton, quarks**.

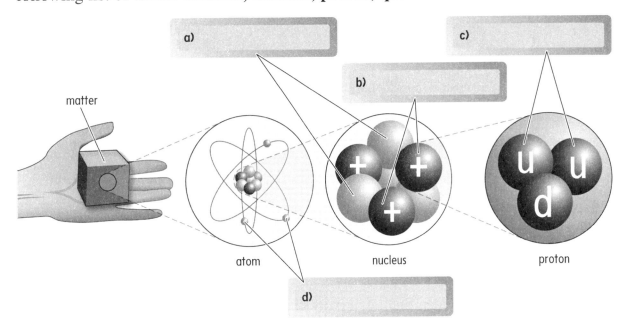

matter   atom   nucleus   proton

2.4 Assessment

Match each description on the left with the person on the right. Each person may be used **more than once**.

Description	Person
1. _____ rejected Democritus's idea of empty space	A. Bohr
2. _____ proposed that electrons exist in energy levels	B. Dalton
3. _____ said that atoms cannot be created or destroyed	C. Aristotle
4. _____ proposed that protons and neutrons have the same mass	D. Thomson
5. _____ suggested that electrons have a certain amount of energy	E. Chadwick
6. _____ discovered that electrons are negatively charged particles	F. Rutherford
7. _____ discovered that the nucleus is the dense centre of the atom	
8. _____ discovered that neutrons are particles with a neutral charge	
9. _____ suggested that the nucleus accounts for most of the atom's mass	

Circle the letter of the best answer for questions 10 to 21.

10. Who was the first to introduce the idea that matter was made of atoms?

A. Bohr   **C.** Rutherford

B. Aristotle   **D.** Democritus

11. Who proposed the idea that negatively charged electrons are embedded in a positively charged ball as shown in the diagram?

A. Bohr

B. Dalton

C. Rutherford

D. Thomson

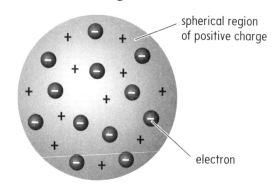

spherical region of positive charge

electron

12. The current modern atomic model suggests that

    A. electrons are found in the nucleus

    B. electrons exist as clouds of electric charge

    C. electrons exist within a large positive sphere

    D. electrons are found in circular distinct energy shells around the nucleus

13. The nucleus of an atom contains

    A. protons and neutrons

    B. protons and electrons

    C. electrons and neutrons

    D. electrons, protons, and neutrons

14. Which of the following correctly matches the subatomic particle with its charge and location in an atom?

	Subatomic Particle	Charge	Location
A.	Proton	Positive	Energy level
B.	Neutron	Negative	Nucleus
C.	Neutron	Neutral	Nucleus
D.	Electron	Neutral	Energy level

Use the following diagram of an atom to answer questions 15 to 19.

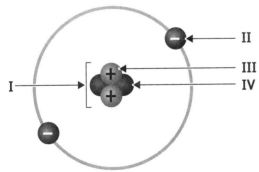

15. Which labelled part in the diagram represents a proton?

    A. I

    B. II

    C. III

    D. IV

16. Which of the following is the structure labelled IV in the diagram?

   A. proton

   B. neutron

   C. electron

   D. nucleus

17. Which of the following exists in energy levels?

   A. I

   B. II

   C. III

   D. IV

18. What is the charge of the structure labelled I?

   A. neutral charge

   B. positive charge

   C. negative charge

   D. it depends on the element

19. Which two subatomic particles have charges that are opposite to each other?

   A. I and II

   B. II and III

   C. II and IV

   D. III and IV

20. What are examples of composite particles?

   A. protons and neutrons

   B. protons and electrons

   C. neutrons and electrons

   D. protons, neutrons, and electrons

21. Which of the following statements is correct?

A. The kinetic molecular theory and the atomic theory both describe the composition and behaviour of matter.

B. The kinetic molecular theory and the atomic theory are the same thing.

C. The kinetic molecular theory and the atomic theory both explain the composition and behaviour of matter.

D. The kinetic molecular theory and the atomic theory are models for the composition and behaviour of matter.

22. Complete the following T-chart to compare a proton to an electron.

T-Chart Graphic Organizer	
Proton	**Electron**
Composite particle	
	Negatively charged
Found in nucleus	
	Relative mass = 1
Consists of quarks	

What do engineers have to take into account when building a bridge?

What's the Issue?

As part of the largest highway construction project in British Columbia's history, the Ministry of Transportation spent $3.3 billion to build the new Port Mann Bridge. The goal was to decrease traffic congestion and help traffic flow more easily. An estimated 100 000 to 115 000 motorists cross the bridge every day. The bridge connects Surrey to Coquitlam, and it is financed entirely by tolls. The new structure is the second-longest cable-stayed bridge in North America. It spans 2020 m across the Fraser River. At 65 m wide, it is the second-widest bridge in the world. It has 10 lanes of traffic and a 5 m multi-use path for pedestrians and cyclists.

The bridge has 288 steel suspension cables that run from two 75-m-high pylon towers to the bridge deck. The steel cables are very strong to provide support. Massive amounts of rebar, structural steel, and asphalt were used for the bridge deck. As with any modern bridge, reinforced concrete was used because it is inexpensive, yet strong.

Steel and concrete are ideal to use together because the degree to which they expand with temperature changes is nearly the same. There are also expansion joints in the bridge to help prevent damage to the overall structure of the bridge from thermal expansion and contraction.

In December 2012, massive chunks of ice collected on the cold suspension cables. As the air temperature began to warm up, the ice started to melt. The high winds then knocked these ice chunks off the cables, and they dropped like ice bombs to the car deck below. More than 100 vehicles were damaged. Experts believe that the cold temperatures, precipitation, air moisture, and strong winds all played a role in such large pieces of ice forming on the cables of the bridge.

Engineers were hired to winter-proof the Port Mann Bridge.

- ◆ They sprayed the cables with a coating that repels water.
- ◆ They installed custom-designed cable sweepers that travel along the cables to prevent the buildup of ice and snow.
- ◆ A de-icing spray was applied to the bridge.

As a result of these steps, the problem was solved.

Dig Deeper

Collaborate with your classmates to explore one or more of these questions—or generate your own questions to explore.

1. How do engineers decide what type of bridge to build? Find out the process of designing and constructing a bridge.

2. What are some physical and chemical properties that engineers consider when choosing the best materials to build bridges? Why is it important to think about these properties?

3. Research the physical and chemical properties of concrete and steel. Find out the different uses for these materials. How do their properties relate to the ways industries use them?

4. What other materials can be used to build bridges? Are there more eco-friendly choices? What are the advantages and disadvantages of using the different materials?

5. How long would you expect a bridge like the Port Mann Bridge to last, considering the open exposure to weather and wet conditions?

6. How do weather conditions and changes in temperature affect the structural integrity of bridges? Would engineers have to consider different issues if a bridge like the Port Mann Bridge were built in Prince George, B.C., where there are severe winters, freezing temperatures, and lots of precipitation?

7. Imagine you are on the engineering team that was asked to provide solutions for winter-proofing the Port Mann Bridge. Research other suggestions to present to the Ministry of Transportation.

How does electromagnetic radiation shape your world?

Use with textbook pages 186–201.

 *Create a Quiz*

After reading this page, create a five-question quiz based on what you have learned. Trade your quiz with a partner, and answer the questions.

An Introduction to Electromagnetic Radiation

Electromagnetic radiation is a form of energy. There are seven types of electromagnetic radiation:

- radio waves
- microwaves
- infrared radiation
- visible light
- ultraviolet radiation
- X-rays
- gamma rays

Sources of Electromagnetic Radiation

- The Sun gives off all types of electromagnetic radiation. The energy carried by this radiation is produced by nuclear reactions.

- Chemical reactions in living things can give off visible light.

- All objects, including you, give off infrared radiation. We sense infrared radiation as heat. If objects are very hot, they give off visible light too.

- A cell phone is a source of microwaves. Commercial radio stations send out radio wave signals.

- X-rays are produced by a change in the speed of very fast-moving electrons in an X-ray tube.

- Radioisotopes are atoms with unstable nuclei. Iodine-131 is a radioisotope that gives off gamma rays.

Applications of Electromagnetic Radiation

- Electromagnetic radiation and technologies such as luminol and infrared photography help criminal investigators find evidence that is invisible to the unaided eye.

- Radio waves and magnets work together in magnetic resonance imaging (MRI) to help doctors diagnose disease.

- X-ray imaging is useful for diagnosing conditions like broken bones and cavities in teeth.

- Satellites above Earth's surface use different types of electromagnetic radiation to gather information about our planet.

- Electromagnetic radiation is used to study the universe through tools such as the Hubble Space Telescope and the Very Large Array radio telescope on Earth.

 *Reading Check*

Describe a way that medical professionals use electromagnetic radiation.

To help medical professionals with diagnosing diseases such as cancer.

Electromagnetic Radiation Applications

Use with textbook pages 188–189.

Write a use for each type of electromagnetic radiation listed below. In the box, draw a picture to illustrate your example.

1. X-rays

Use: Find cracked bones

2. Radio Waves

Use: Help diagnose disease

3. Gamma Rays

Use: Television

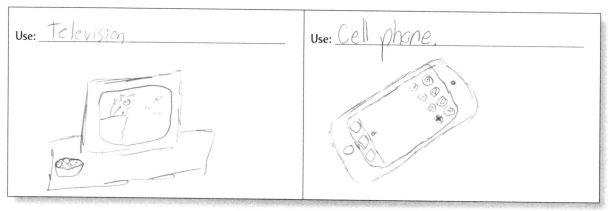

4. Microwaves

Use: Cell phone.

5. Infrared Radiation

Use: Solar pannel

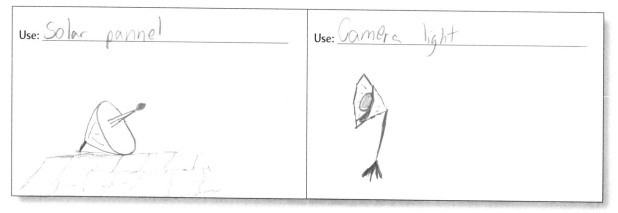

6. Ultraviolet Radiation

Use: Camera light

How Does Electromagnetic Radiation Shape Your World?

Use with textbook pages 186–201.

Label the different types of electromagnetic radiation that you can see used in the illustration below. Use the list of words given below the illustration.

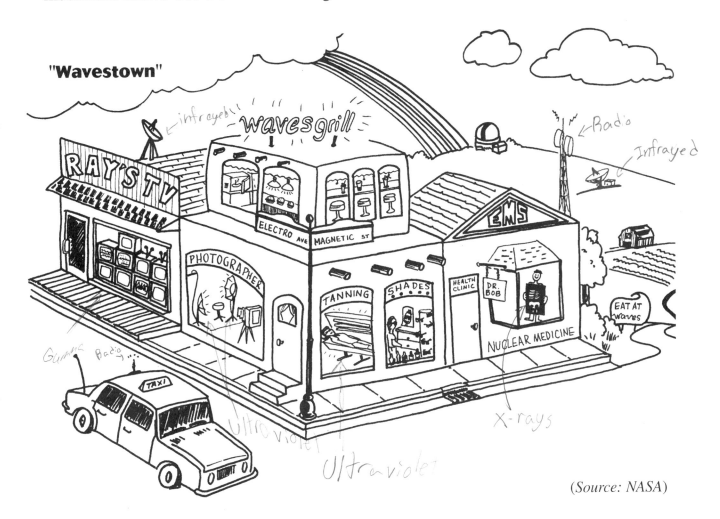

"**Wavestown**"

(Source: NASA)

Vocabulary

X-rays	radio waves	gamma rays
visible light	microwaves	infrared radiation
		ultraviolet radiation

Using Electromagnetic Radiation to See Our World

Use with textbook pages 186–201.

Complete the table below. List the type of electromagnetic radiation used by each technology, and briefly describe how it works. The first one is done for you.

	Technology	Electromagnetic Radiation Used	How It Works
1.	Using luminol to solve crimes	Visible light	Gives off visible light when in contact with iron in blood.
2.	Radios		
3.	Weather satellites		
4.	Texting on cell phones		
5.	Detecting cavities in teeth		
6.	Magnetic resonance imaging (MRI)		

Electromagnetic Radiation: Plus, Minus, and Interesting

Use with textbook pages 186-201.

1. Identify the type(s) of electromagnetic radiation associated with each source listed below.

   a) Sun _____

   b) human being _____

   c) light bulb _____

   d) cell phone _____

   e) Iodine-131 _____

   f) communication system used by police _____

2. Use the PMI chart below to list some helpful and harmful effects of electromagnetic radiation as well as some interesting facts you have learned.

Electromagnetic Radiation Affects Our Daily Lives		
P (Plus)	M (Minus)	I (Interesting)

3.1 Assessment

Match each term on the left with the best descriptor on the right. Each descriptor may be used only once.

Term	Descriptor
1. _E_ X-rays	A. used to send radio broadcasts
2. _C_ microwaves	B. used in night vision cameras
3. _D_ gamma rays	C. used to send text messages
4. _A_ radio waves	D. used to kill cancer cells
5. _B_ infrared radiation	E. used by the dentist to take pictures of your teeth

Circle the letter of the best answer for questions 6 to 12.

6. Which of the following types of radiation is responsible for causing skin cancer?

   A. visible light   **C.** ultraviolet radiation

   B. infrared radiation   **D.** gamma rays

7. Which of the following is a benefit of of ultraviolet radiation?

   A. improves eyesight

   B. helps make vitamin D

   C. helps make vitamin E

   D. reduces effects of aging

8. Which of the following types of electromagnetic radiation can be given off by objects in outer space?

I	X-rays
II	microwaves
III	radio waves

   A. I and II only

   B. I and III only

   C. II and III only

   D. I, II, and III

9. Which of the following types of electromagnetic radiation could help an investigator determine whether a painting is fake?

I	X-rays
II	infrared radiation
III	ultraviolet radiation

 A. I and II only

 B. I and III only

 C. II and III only

 D. I, II, and III

10. Which two kinds of electromagnetic radiation are given off by a campfire?

 A. visible light and microwaves

 B. visible light and infrared radiation

 C. infrared radiation and microwaves

 D. ultraviolet radiation and infrared radiation

11. Which two types of electromagnetic radiation do satellites use to monitor weather conditions?

 A. X-rays and gamma rays

 B. visible light and infrared radiation

 C. ultraviolet radiation and visible light

 D. radio waves and ultraviolet radiation

12. Which of the following generates X-rays?

 A. a cell phone

 B. an X-ray tube

 C. a halogen bulb

 D. all of the above

13. Complete the following mind map. Give some examples of what would happen if the Sun did not rise.

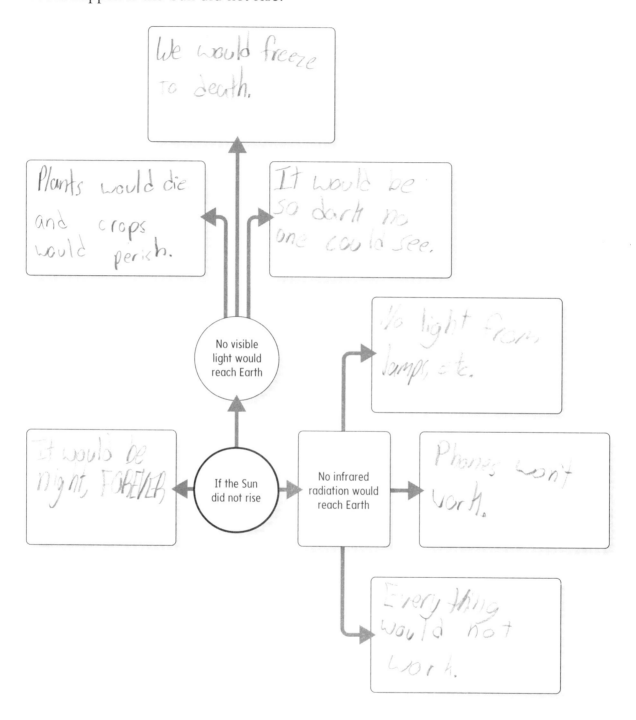

We would freeze to death.

Plants would die and crops would perish.

It would be so dark no one could see.

No visible light would reach Earth

No light from lamps, etc.

It would be night, FOREVER

If the Sun did not rise

No infrared radiation would reach Earth

Phones won't work.

Everything would not work.

How can models explain the properties of electromagnetic radiation?

Use with textbook pages 202–219.

Visible light can be used as a model for all types of electromagnetic radiation. Scientists use three models to show the properties of visible light and other types of electromagnetic radiation.

The Ray Model of Light

The **ray model of light** is used to show that light travels in a straight-line path. A ray is an arrow that indicates the direction in which light is travelling.

The ray model of light can be used to

- show that an object casts a sharp-edged shadow on the wall, because light cannot travel around it.

- predict the location, size, and shape of shadows.

- show that light rays spread out as they travel from a light source, causing light to get dimmer as it travels.

The Wave Model of Light

The **wave model of light** is part of a theory that explains that light has wave-like properties. In the 1800s, Thomas Young's experiment showed that light spreads out into a series of lines when it passes through two narrow slits. This pattern of lines could only be explained if light has wave-like properties.

Light waves have a wavelength, amplitude, and frequency.

- **Wavelength** is the distance from one crest (or trough) of a wave to the next crest (or trough). The colours of the visible light spectrum are different wavelengths of light. Red has the longest wavelength. Violet has the shortest.

- **Amplitude** is the distance from the centre line to the crest or trough of a wave.

- **Frequency** is the number of complete wavelengths that pass a point in one second as a wave goes by. As wavelength decreases, frequency increases. As wavelength increases, frequency decreases.

 *Identify Details*

Use a highlighter to mark all the details about how models show the properties of electromagnetic radiation.

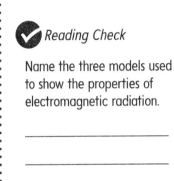 *Reading Check*

Name the three models used to show the properties of electromagnetic radiation.

_____

_____

_____

✓ *Reading Check*

Which model of light can
be used to explain the
photoelectric effect?

_____

_____

_____

The Particle Model of Light

The particle model of light is part of a
theory that explains that light has particle-like
properties. Scientist Albert Einstein used this model to
explain the photoelectric effect.

The Photoelectric Effect

- Different colours of light shine onto a certain metal.
  Electrons are never given off when energy from red light
  hits the metal.

- Electrons are always given off when energy from blue
  light hits the metal.

The wave model of light cannot explain the photoelectric
effect, but the particle model of light can.

Einstein's Explanation:

Einstein realized that light acts like a particle (called a
photon) when an object absorbs its energy. Each photon
carries an exact amount of energy. Photons carry more energy
as the frequency of electromagnetic radiation increases and
wavelength decreases.

- Red light has a lower frequency and a longer wavelength,
  so photons of red light carry less energy. They do not
  carry enough energy to make the metal give off electrons.

- Blue light has a higher frequency and a shorter
  wavelength, so photons of blue light carry more energy.
  They carry enough energy to make the metal give off
  electrons.

Making Sense of Models

Use with textbook pages 202–219.

A model is a representation of "something." It can be a statement, a chart, an equation, a picture, or an imagined image that makes it easier to understand the "something." For each situation below, describe or draw an example of a model.

1. A model that helps you show something that is too large to see all at once. *The building is too high to see.*	**3.** A model that represents data or information. *Broken Bone - Left thigh* *Information about a broken bone.*
2. A model that shows an object that is too small to see with the unaided eye. *Machine* *Eye* *The machine can see the germs but the unaided eye can't.*	**4.** A model that helps you show something that cannot be seen otherwise. *The machine can show the wavelengths.*

Young's Experiment

Use with textbook pages 207-208.

Use the diagram below to describe Thomas Young's experiment in your own words. Then use your description to answer the question that follows.

Light source

1. _____
   _____
   _____

2. _____
   _____
   _____

3. _____
   _____
   _____
   _____
   _____
   _____

4. Explain how Young's experiment supported the idea of a wave model of light.

_____

_____

_____

_____

Parts of a Wave

Use with textbook page 209.

Use the following vocabulary words to label the parts of a wave.

Vocabulary
amplitude
crest
trough
wavelength

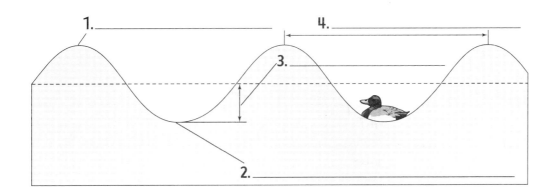

1. _____ 4. _____

3. _____

2. _____

5. Describe the wave features listed below.

a) amplitude

_____

_____

b) crest

_____

_____

c) trough

_____

_____

d) wavelength

_____

_____

Characteristics of Waves

Use with textbook page 209.

Use the information in the graphs to answer the questions.

1. How long is the wavelength of the wave shown below? _____

2. How large is the amplitude of the wave shown below? _____

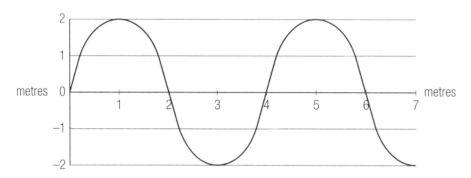

3. Which wave shown below has the smaller amplitude, Wave A or Wave B?

_____

4. How does the frequency compare for Wave A and Wave B? _____

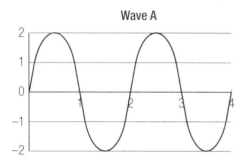
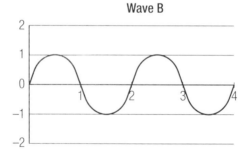

5. What is the same for Waves X and Y shown below: amplitude, wavelength, or frequency? _____

6. Which wave has a greater frequency, Wave X or Wave Y? _____

7. Which wave has a longer wavelength, Wave X or Wave Y? _____

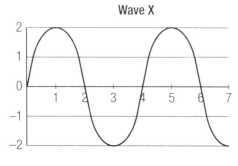
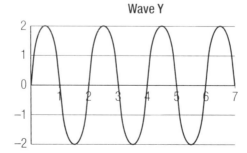

Another Thought Experiment

Use with textbook pages 211–212.

Have you ever seen a "strength-testing" device like the one shown here? Only those people with strength that exceeds a minimum level can strike the target hard enough to ring the bell. Weaker contestants cannot ring the bell, no matter how many times they strike the target. So a lot of weak strikes do not have the same effect as a single hard strike.

For this "strength-testing" device, everyone uses the same hammer. The only variable is the strength of the contestants. But what if the weight of the hammer varied instead? How would that affect the ringing of the bell? Study the two diagrams shown below, and answer the questions to see how the bell-ringing effect compares with the particle model and photoelectric effect.

1. In this analogy, what does the hammer represent?

_____

_____

2. What does the "bell-ringing effect" represent?

_____

_____

3. Which hammer delivers more energy? Explain your reasoning.

_____

_____

4. Which photon delivers more energy? Explain your reasoning.

_____

_____

5. Using the diagrams, predict which one represents red light and which one represents blue light. Explain your reasoning.

_____

_____

6. According to the wave model, which has the longer wavelength: blue light or red light?

_____

_____

7. According to the particle model, which has more energy: blue light or red light? Explain your reasoning.

_____

_____

3.2 Assessment

Match each term on the left with the best descriptor on the right. Each descriptor may be used only once.

Term	Descriptor
1. ____ crest	A. a particle of light or other type of electromagnetic radiation
2. ____ trough	B. the lowest point of a wave
3. ____ photon	C. the highest point of a wave
4. ____ amplitude	D. distance from trough to trough
5. ____ frequency	E. height of crest from the centre line of the wave
6. ____ wavelength	F. number of complete wavelengths that pass a point in one second

Circle the letter of the best answer for questions 7 to 17.

7. Which statement(s) about electromagnetic radiation is (are) true?

A. All types of electromagnetic radiation can travel through empty space.

B. All types of electromagnetic radiation are invisible as they travel through empty space.

C. All types of electromagnetic radiation travel at the same speed through empty space.

D. all of the above

8. Why is visible light used to model all types of electromagnetic radiation?

A. It is fairly easy and safe to study.

B. It becomes visible when it interacts with matter.

C. It has many properties in common with other types of electromagnetic radiation.

D. all of the above

9. The ray model of light depends on the fact that

A. light is made up of photons according to the particle model of light.

B. light is made up of waves according to the wave model of light.

C. light follows a straight-line path as it travels from a source.

D. light gets dimmer as it moves farther from a source.

10. A ray diagram

    A. is a diagram that involves light rays.

    B. can be used to predict the location, size, and shape of shadows.

    C. pictures a light ray as a straight line with an arrow on one end.

    D. all of the above

11. Which of the following is a way to measure a wavelength?

    A. the distance from crest to crest

    B. the distance from trough to centre line

    C. the distance from the top of a crest to the bottom of a trough

    D. the distance covered by one wave in 1 s

Use the following diagrams to answer questions 12 and 13.

Wave X

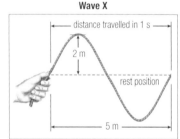

Wave Y

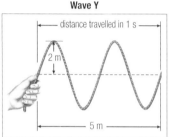

12. Wave X has a longer wavelength than Wave Y.

    A. The statement is supported by the diagrams.

    B. The statement is not supported by the diagrams.

    C. You cannot tell by looking at the diagrams.

13. Which statement is correct?

    A. Both Wave X and Wave Y have the same amplitude.

    B. Both Wave X and Wave Y have the same wavelength.

    C. Both Wave X and Wave Y have the same frequency and wavelength.

    D. Neither amplitude nor wavelength is the same for both Wave X and Wave Y.

14. Which colour of visible light has the shortest wavelength?

    A. red   **C.** yellow

    B. violet   **D.** orange

15. Which of the following statements about photons is true?

A. Each photon carries variable amounts of energy.

B. Photons carry more energy as the frequency of electromagnetic radiation decreases.

C. Photons carry more energy as the wavelength of electromagnetic energy decreases.

D. None of these statements is true.

16. Which of the following statements about blue and red light is true?

A. Photons of blue light carry more energy than photons of red light.

B. Blue light has a lower frequency and a shorter wavelength than red light.

C. Blue light has a higher frequency and a longer wavelength than red light.

D. Photons of blue light carry less energy than photons of red light.

17. Which models are needed to explain the properties of light?

A. the particle model of light and the wave model of light

B. the particle model of light, the wave model of light, and the ray model of light

C. the particle model of light and the ray model of light

D. the wave model of light and the ray model of light

18. Complete the following concept map for the three models of visible light.

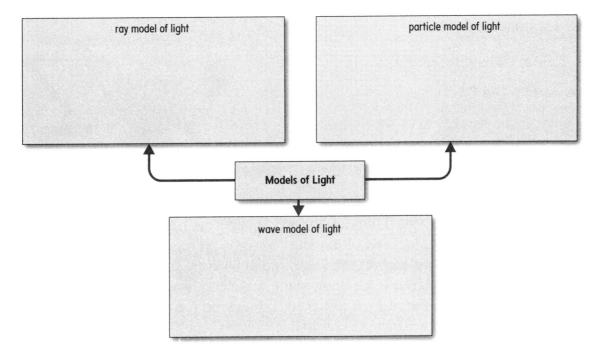

How does light behave when it encounters different materials and surfaces?

Use with textbook pages 220–229.

Identify Definitions

Highlight the definition of each key word in bold type in this summary.

Light interacts with different materials and surfaces in different ways. Light may reflect, be absorbed, be transmitted, or refract.

When light **reflects**, it "bounces off" a surface and changes direction. There are two different types of reflection. These are described below.

Reflection off a smooth surface (such as a mirror)	• Produces a clear image (a likeness) of the viewer and the surroundings. • The pattern of reflected rays is very similar to the pattern of the incoming rays. That is why you can see an image when the light reaches your eyes. 
Reflection off a rough surface (such as paper)	• Does not produce an image. • The pattern of reflected rays is no longer similar to the pattern of the incoming rays, so no image appears on the paper. However, some reflected rays do reach your eyes. That is why you can see the paper. 

Reading Check

Explain why you see a blue letter as blue.

Blue letters absorves all wave lengths that aren't blue so only blue light reaches your eyes.

When light is **absorbed**, its energy is trapped in an object as heat. Think of a piece of paper with a black letter on it. The black ink of the letter absorbs all incoming light. No rays reflect off the letter into your eyes, so it looks black. If the letter is a colour, some wavelengths of light are absorbed, and the rest are reflected. For example, a blue letter absorbs all wavelengths of visible light except blue. Only the blue light reaches your eyes.

Transmission

Some materials let different amounts of light pass through them. When light passes through a material, the light is **transmitted**. The material that light passes through is called a *medium*. Different materials transmit different amounts of light. For example, clear glass transmits more light than paper.

Refraction

Light travels in the same direction when it travels through a medium. When light enters a different medium, it changes direction. This change of direction is called **refraction**.

Transparent, Translucent, and Opaque Materials

A material can be described based on how much light it lets pass through.

 Reading Check

How does light behave when it enters a different medium?

Transparent lets almost all light pass. Translucent lets most light pass but it's scattered. Opaque dosen't let any light pass through.

Transparent Materials	Translucent Materials	Opaque Materials
• Transmit almost all light. • Objects can be seen clearly through them. • Examples: clear glass, plastic, water, and air	• Let most light pass through, but light is scattered in many directions. • Objects seen through them are blurry. • Examples: frosted plastic, waxed paper	• Reflect and absorb light. • Let no light pass through. • Objects cannot be seen through them. • Examples: wood, metal, and stone

Classifying Materials

Use with textbook page 225.

Objects can either be transparent, translucent, or opaque, as shown in the diagram below.

TRANSPARENT

TRANSLUCENT

OPAQUE

1. Use the diagram above to help you identify whether each of the following materials is transparent, translucent, or opaque.

   a) frosted bathroom window _Translucent_

   b) water _Transparent_

   c) t-shirt _Opaque_

   d) stainless steel spoon _Opaque_

   e) clear glass window _Transparent_

   f) light bulb _Transparent, Translucent - Depends what type_

   g) duct tape _Opaque_

   h) paper lunch bag _Opaque_

   i) your hand _Opaque_

   j) cardboard _Opaque_

   k) wood door _Opaque_

   l) sunglasses _Translucent_

   m) paper towel _Opaque_

   n) eye glasses _Opaque_

   o) concrete wall _Opaque_

   p) tissue paper _Opaque_

How Light Behaves

Use with textbook pages 220–229.

1. Complete the following table.

Materials	How much light does the material let pass through?	How does the light behave?	Can you see through this material?	Examples of Materials
Transparent	Almost All	Stays Straight	Yes, clear	1. Light bulb 2. Water at Hawii
Translucent	Most	Bounces Around	Yes, blurry	1. Light bulb 2. Sunglasses
Opaque	None	Bounces Around	No, not at all	1. Metal locker 2. Cardboard box

2. Label the diagram shown below. State whether light is mostly absorbed, reflected, transmitted, or scattered by each object in the illustration.

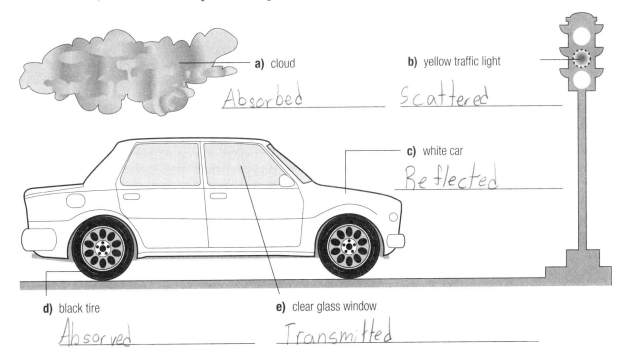

a) cloud

Absorbed

b) yellow traffic light

Scattered

c) white car

Reflected

d) black tire

Absorved

e) clear glass window

Transmitted

3.3 Assessment

Match each term on the left with the best descriptor on the right. Each descriptor may be used only once.

Term	Descriptor
1. _D_ reflection	A. This occurs as light passes through an object.
2. _C_ refraction	B. The process in which light changes direction as it travels from one medium into another.
3. _B_ scattering	C. This occurs when light bounces off a surface and travels in another direction.
4. _E_ absorption	D. Responsible for dark surfaces getting hot on sunny days.
5. _A_ transmission	E. Reason why objects seen through translucent materials are blurry.

Circle the letter of the best answer for questions 6 to 14.

6. Which of the following objects will transmit the most light?

    A. a clear glass window   **C.** a piece of wood

    B. a chunk of gold   **D.** a white piece of paper

7. Which of the following objects will absorb the most light?

    A. sunglasses   **C.** a white stone

    B. a black hockey puck   **D.** a clear plastic bag

8. Which of the following objects is the least opaque?

    A. a tent   **C.** a plastic sandwich bag

    B. a granite counter top   **D.** a fabric shower curtain

9. A pencil in a glass half full of water appears broken at the water line due to which process?

    A. reflection   **C.** absorption

    B. refraction   **D.** transmission

Use the following diagram to answer questions 10 to 13.

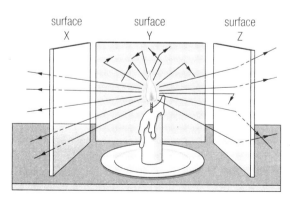

surface X   surface Y   surface Z

10. Which of the surfaces is transparent?

A. Surface X

B. Surface Y

C. Surface Z

D. Surface Y and Surface Z

11. Which of the surfaces transmits the fewest light rays?

A. Surface X

B. Surface Y

C. Surface Z

D. Surface X and Surface Z

12. Which of the surfaces is most likely made of frosted plastic or glass?

A. Surface X

B. Surface Y

C. Surface Z

D. Surface X and Surface Y

13. Which statement correctly describes Surface Y?

A. It transmits all light.

B. It scatters all light.

C. It absorbs all light.

D. It allows no light to pass through it.

14. Which of the following processes is shown in the diagram on the right?

A. refraction

B. reflection

C. absorption

D. transmission

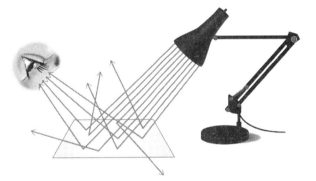

15. Complete a spider chart/map for the different ways that light interacts with different materials and surfaces. The graphic organizer has been partially completed to help guide you.

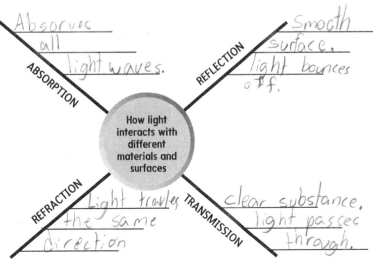

ABSORPTION — Absorbes all light waves.

REFLECTION — Smooth surface. light bounces off.

REFRACTION — Light travles the same direction

TRANSMISSION — clear substance. light passes through.

How light interacts with different materials and surfaces

How does light behave when it is reflected?

Use with textbook pages 230–245.

Create Flashcards

Write a question that might be on a test on one side of a flashcard. Write the answer on the other side. Complete at least five cards. Then exchange cards with a partner and quiz yourself until you get all the answers correct.

Reading Check

According to the laws of reflection, where are the reflected ray and the incident ray located with respect to the normal?

_____

_____

_____

_____

Reading Check

Which mirrors form misshapen images?

_____

_____

_____

The Laws of Reflection

Light rays always follow a predictable path when they reflect from a surface. The **laws of reflection** determine this path.

Law	Key Words
• The angle of reflection (r) is equal to the angle of incidence (i).	**reflected ray**: the light ray that has bounced off a reflecting surface
• The reflected ray and the incident ray are on opposite sides of the normal.	**incident ray**: the light ray that travels toward the reflecting surface
• The incident ray, the normal, and the reflected ray lie on the same plane.	**angle of incidence**: the angle between the incident ray and the normal
	angle of reflection: the angle between the reflected ray and the normal
	normal: a line perpendicular to a surface such as a mirror
	plane: flat surface

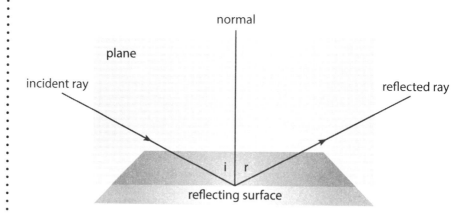

Reflections in Mirrors

Light produces different images when it reflects off mirrors of different shapes. Images can be real or virtual. **Real images** form when reflected rays meet. These images are visible in front of the mirror. **Virtual images** form when reflected rays do not actually meet; only the extended rays do. These images appear to be behind the mirror.

Shape of Mirror	Behaviour of Light	Characteristics of Image
plane mirror an extremely smooth, flat reflective surface	• Light rays reflecting off an object follow the laws of reflection and reflect backwards off the mirror. • Rays that reach a viewer's eyes carry the same pattern of light that was reflected off the object. • The brain assumes light travels in a straight line and thinks the image is behind the mirror. object plane mirror image	• same size as the object • same distance from the mirror as the object • upright • virtual • reversed compared to the object
concave mirror a mirror with a reflecting surface that curves inward	• Light rays follow the laws of reflection. They come together or converge at a single point, called a focal point, after they reflect off the mirror. focal point	Depending on where the object is located, the image: • may be smaller or larger than the object • may be real or virtual • may be upright or inverted • may appear closer to or farther from the mirror than the object The image is always misshapen.
convex mirror a mirror with a reflecting surface that curves outward	• Light rays follow the laws of reflection. They spread apart or diverge after they reflect off the mirror. focal point	• smaller than the object • closer to the mirror than the object • upright • virtual The image is always misshapen.

Practice with Protractors

Use with textbook pages 230–245.

If you are asked to draw light rays in models, it is important to draw the lines accurately. For this reason, you will need to use a protractor properly.

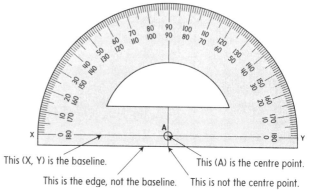

This (X, Y) is the baseline.
This is the edge, not the baseline.
This (A) is the centre point.
This is not the centre point.

- Position the protractor carefully.

- The baseline (XY) lines up with the starting arm of the angle.

- The protractor's centre point (A) must match the vertex (corner) of the angle.

- Look straight down on the scale to get an accurate reading of the number of degrees.

1. Use a protractor to measure, in degrees, each of the angles shown below.

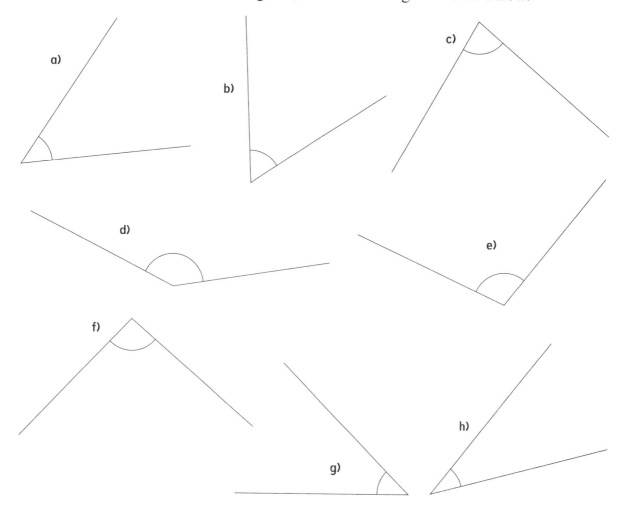

How Do the Images Formed in Mirrors Compare?

Use with textbook pages 230–245.

All mirrors form images of objects because mirrors reflect the light that strikes them in a regular pattern. How the image looks depends on whether the mirror is flat or curved. Complete the following chart to compare the different types of mirrors.

	Plane Mirror	Concave Mirror	Convex Mirror
Is the reflecting surface of the mirror flat, curved inward, or curved outward?			
Is the image smaller, larger, or the same size as the object?			
Is the image upright or upside down?			
Is the image misshapen?			
Does the image seem to be behind the mirror or in front of the mirror?			
Give one example of how this type of mirror might be used.			

Looking into Mirrors

Use with textbook pages 230–245.

Fill in the chart below.

- Identify whether the mirror is a plane, convex, or concave. If you cannot tell from the diagram, try to infer its shape from its function.
- Briefly explain why you think this type of mirror is used for the function indicated.

1. full-length mirror in a dressing room	5. store security mirror
2. make-up mirror	6. car side-view mirror
3. car rear-view mirror	7. mirror in flashlight
4. dental mirror	8. shaving mirror

3.4 Assessment

Match each term on the left with the best descriptor on the right. Each descriptor may be used only once.

Term	Descriptor
1. _____ normal	A. extremely smooth, flat reflective surface
2. _____ incident ray	B. light ray going toward a mirror
3. _____ reflected ray	C. light ray that bounces off a mirror
4. _____ focal point	D. angle between the incident ray and the normal
5. _____ plane mirror	E. angle between the reflected ray and the normal
6. _____ angle of reflection	F. line perpendicular to a surface, such as a mirror
7. _____ angle of incidence	G. point where light rays come together when they reflect off a concave mirror

Circle the letter of the best answer for questions 8 to 17.

8. Which of the following mirrors can be used to make an image that is the same size as the object?

 A. plane mirror

 B. convex mirror

 C. concave mirror

 D. both concave and convex mirrors

9. What do all three types of mirrors have in common?

 A. They all produce upside-down images.

 B. They all reflect light rays to form an image.

 C. They all reflect light rays so that the rays diverge and do not meet.

 D. They all reflect light rays so that the rays converge on a focal point.

10. What shape of mirror would you use if you wanted the image to be larger than the object?

 A. plane mirror

 B. convex mirror

 C. concave mirror

 D. no mirror produces an image that is larger than the object

11. Which of the following statements about a plane mirror is incorrect?

  A. It produces an upright image.

  B. It produces an image in front of the mirror.

  C. It produces an image that is the same size as the object.

  D. It produces an image that appears to be the same distance from the mirror as the object.

12. Which of the following lie on the same plane?

I	normal
II	incident ray
III	reflected ray

  A. I and II only

  B. I and III only

  C. II and III only

  D. I, II, and III

13. If the angle of incidence of a light ray striking a smooth, flat mirror is 50°, what is the angle of reflection?

  A. 5°

  B. 25°

  C. 50°

  D. 100°

14. Which of the following describes the difference between a virtual image and a real image?

	Virtual Image	Real Image
A.	Appears to be behind the mirror	Located in front of the mirror
B.	Located in front of the mirror	Appears to be behind the mirror
C.	Forms when reflected rays meet	Forms when extended rays meet
D.	Forms when incident rays meet	Forms when refracted rays meet

15. An object that is 10 cm high is placed 20 cm from a plane mirror. Which of the following describes the image formed in the plane mirror?

  A. The image is 20 cm high and 10 cm from the mirror. The image is upright.

  B. The image is 10 cm high and 20 cm from the mirror. The image is upright.

  C. The image is 20 cm high and 10 cm from the mirror. The image is upside-down.

  D. The image is 10 cm high and 20 cm from the mirror. The image is upside-down.

16. Which of the following identifies the types of mirrors associated with the bowl (the inner surface) and the back of a spoon?

	Bowl of a Spoon	Back of a Spoon
A.	Plane mirror	Convex mirror
B.	Convex mirror	Concave mirror
C.	Concave mirror	Convex mirror
D.	Concave mirror	Plane mirror

17. Which of the following are characteristics of reflections in convex mirrors?

I	Image is upside down
II	Image is a virtual image
III	Image is smaller than the object

A. I and II only

B. I and III only

C. II and III only

D. I, II, and III

18. Complete the Venn diagram to compare and contrast a concave mirror, a convex mirror, and a plane mirror.

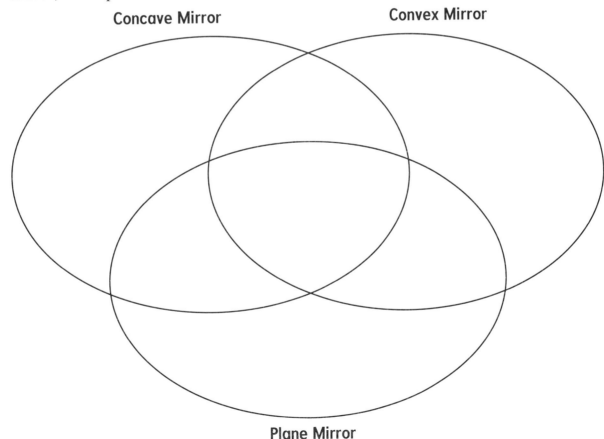

Concave Mirror

Convex Mirror

Plane Mirror

How does light behave when it moves from one medium to another?

Use with textbook pages 246-259.

 In Your Own Words

Highlight the main ideas in this summary. Then rewrite each main idea in your own words.

 *Reading Check*

Why does light change speed and direction when it travels from one medium to another?

_____

_____

_____

Visualizing Refraction

Light refracts, or changes direction, when it moves from one medium to another. This happens because light travels at different speeds in different media. As light changes speed, the direction it travels in also changes.

Light travels more slowly in a more dense medium than in a less dense medium.

- When light travels from a medium that is less dense to a medium that is more dense, the ray bends toward the normal.

- When light travels from a medium that is more dense to a medium that is less dense, the ray bends away from the normal.

Lenses and Refraction

A **lens** is a transparent object that causes light to refract and has at least one curved side.

- A **converging lens** brings parallel light rays toward a common point. The lens has one or two convex surfaces. A converging lens is thicker in the centre.

- A **diverging lens** causes parallel rays to spread away from a common point. The lens has one or two concave surfaces. A diverging lens is thinner in the centre.

Refraction and lenses make image formation in the human eye possible.

Light travels in a straight line from an object or source to the eye. It first travels through the **cornea,** which is a lens in the front of the eye. The cornea causes light rays to converge.

The light strikes the **retina** at the back of the eye and forms an image.

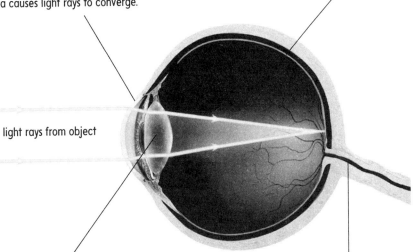

light rays from object

The **lens** also causes light rays to converge. It is responsible for focusing on close objects.

Cells in the retina send nerve impulses to the brain. The brain interprets the impulses as sight.

✓ *Reading Check*

How does refraction make it possible for you to read this question?

_____

_____

_____

Diverging and Converging Lenses

Use with textbook pages 246–261.

Compare and contrast diverging lenses and converging lenses. Complete the graphic organizer shown below.

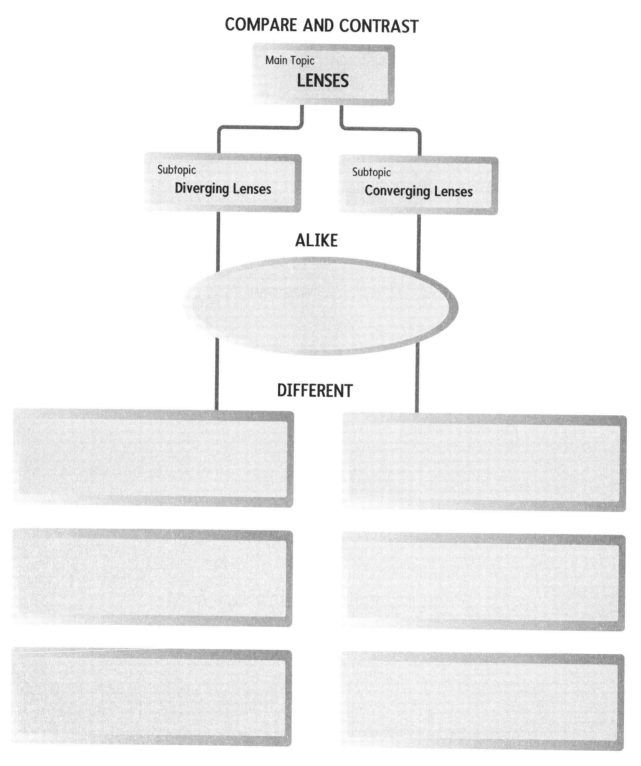

COMPARE AND CONTRAST

Main Topic
LENSES

Subtopic
Diverging Lenses

Subtopic
Converging Lenses

ALIKE

DIFFERENT

The Parts of the Eye

Use with textbook pages 252–253.

Six of the seven statements below are false. Rewrite each false statement to make it true.
Identify the statement that is already true.

1. The lens does most of the focusing of the light rays that pass through the eye.

   _____

   _____

2. The light rays that pass through the eye do not refract.

   _____

   _____

3. The human eye has a diverging lens.

   _____

   _____

4. Incoming light rays first pass through the lens of the eye and then the cornea.

   _____

   _____

5. Light rays are sent to the brain through the optic nerve.

   _____

   _____

6. To focus light from nearby objects, the lens is made shorter and thicker, which makes the lens less curved.

   _____

   _____

7. To focus light from distant objects, the lens keeps its normal shape.

   _____

   _____

An Optical Device to Improve Eyesight

Use with textbook pages 250–255.

What kind of optical device could you design to help improve eyesight? Invent a device that uses lenses and/or mirrors to improve human vision. Be creative. Draw your device below and explain how it works. Add labels to identify the parts.

Putting the Terms Together

Use with textbook pages 184–261.

Complete the following crossword puzzle by using the clues and vocabulary list given.

Vocabulary
absorption
amplitude
concave mirror
convex mirror
converging lens
diverging lens
frequency
laws of
    reflection
lens
particle model
    of light
plane mirror
ray model of light
reflection
refraction
transmission
wavelength
wave model of light

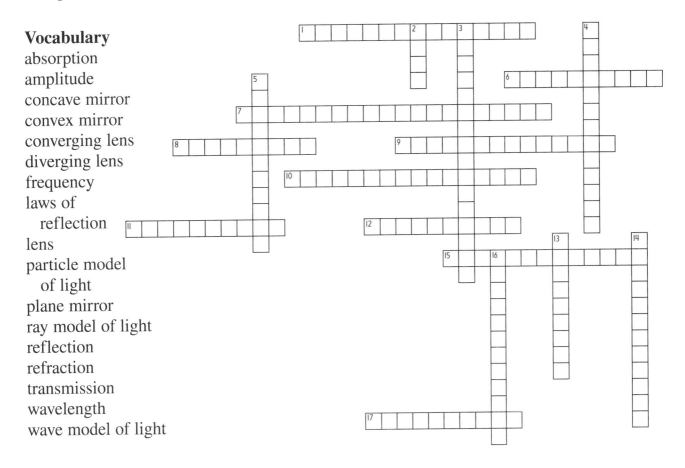

ACROSS

1. idea that light travels in a straight line

6. distance from crest to crest of a wave

7. idea that light has particle-like properties

8. number of wavelengths that pass a point per second

9. refracts light rays toward a common point

10. idea that light has wave-like properties

11. occurs when light bounces off a surface

12. occurs when light changes direction when it travels into a new medium

15. has a reflecting surface curved inward

17. occurs when light energy remains in the object it strikes

DOWN

2. a transparent object that refracts light with at least one curved side

3. three rules describing what happens when light strikes a surface

4. refracts light rays away from each other

5. smooth, flat reflective surface

13. distance from the centre line to the crest of a wave

14. light passes through and keeps travelling

16. has a reflecting surface curved outward

3.5 Assessment

Match each term on the left with the best descriptor on the right. Each descriptor may be used only once.

Term	Descriptor
1. ____ lens	A. bring toward a common point
2. ____ diverge	B. spread away from a common point
3. ____ converge	C. a transparent object that causes light to refract and has a least one curved side
4. ____ diverging lens	D. lens that is thicker in the middle than at the edge
5. ____ converging lens	E. lens that is thinner in the middle than at the edge

Circle the letter of the best answer for questions 6 to 17.

6. Which of the following describes what happens when light moves from air to water?

I	it refracts
II	it changes speed
III	it changes direction

    A. I and II only   **C.** II and III only

    B. I and III only   **D.** I, II, and III

7. Predict what will happen to light when it moves from air (less dense) through a piece of glass (more dense).

    A. It will speed up.   **C.** It will stop moving.

    B. It will slow down.   **D.** Its wavelength will change.

8. Which of the following describes a situation in which light rays bend away from the normal?

    A. When they reflect off plane mirrors with no density.

    B. When they travel through media of the same density.

    C. When they travel from a less dense medium to a more dense medium.

    D. When they travel from a more dense medium to a less dense medium.

9. A lens causes light rays to

    A. stop.   **C.** refract.

    B. multiply.   **D.** bounce back.

10. In a converging lens with two convex sides, light rays refract toward the normal entering the lens and away from the normal leaving the lens. However, the light rays still converge as they leave the lens because of the

    A. density of the lens.

    B. overall shape of the lens.

    C. focal point of the lens.

    D. reflectivity of the lens.

11. What happens to light rays as they pass through a diverging lens?

    A. The lens absorbs them all.

    B. They come together toward a common point.

    C. They spread away from a common point.

    D. They pass through the lens and then reflect back again.

12. Which of the following is true of any lens?

    A. It must have at least one curved side.

    B. It must have two curved sides.

    C. It cannot have any curved sides.

    D. It must be made of glass.

13. Which process makes image formation possible in the human eye?

    A. reflection

    B. refraction

    C. deflection

    D. scattering

14. When light rays enter the eye, they are first refracted by the

    A. lens

    B. retina

    C. cornea

    D. optic nerve

15. Upon which surface is the image formed in the eye?

    A. lens

    B. retina

    C. cornea

    D. optic nerve

16. Which of the following technologies could provide a skier with information about how fast he or she is going down a slope on Big White?

    A. SLR cameras

    B. artificial lenses

    C. heads-up display

    D. wavefront technology

17. Which of the following people would most likely use wavefront technology?

    A. surfer

    B. eye doctor

    C. scuba diver

    D. photographer

18. Complete the following Frayer model diagram for refraction of light rays.

Frayer Model Diagram

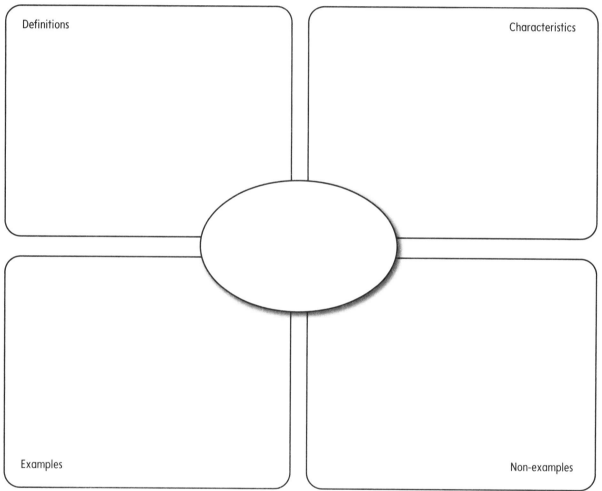

What do we need to know about blue light?

What's the Issue?

If you are like most people, you spend a lot of time in front of one or more types of electronic devices. These can include phones, TVs, tablets, and computers. Digital screens put out all colours of visible light, but they especially put out a lot of blue light. Blue light carries much higher energy than other colours of visible light. In fact, blue light is called high energy visible light, or HEV for short.

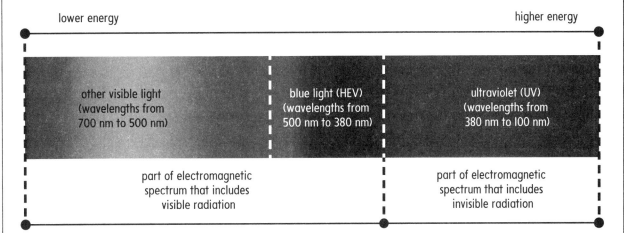

lower energy   higher energy

other visible light
(wavelengths from
700 nm to 500 nm)

blue light (HEV)
(wavelengths from
500 nm to 380 nm)

ultraviolet (UV)
(wavelengths from
380 nm to 100 nm)

part of electromagnetic
spectrum that includes
visible radiation

part of electromagnetic
spectrum that includes
invisible radiation

Blue light is good for you. It provides certain health effects that are beneficial. However, blue light also has effects that can impair health. These effects are associated mostly with the electronic devices that play such a large role in our lives.

Dig Deeper

Collaborate with your classmates to explore one or more of these questions—or generate your own questions to explore.

1. What are the beneficial effects and the negative effects of blue light? How can the same energy be good and bad for you, and what makes the difference?

2. What technologies can support the positive aspects of blue light? What technologies have been developed to protect against the negative aspects?

3. How are the concepts of biological clocks and circadian rhythms connected with blue light?

4. How do the effects (positive and negative) of blue light compare with those of ultraviolet?

What ideas, observations, and evidence led to the theory of plate tectonics?

Use with textbook pages 272–287.

 *Check for Understanding*

As you read, stop and reread any parts you do not understand. Highlight all the sentences that help you get a better understanding.

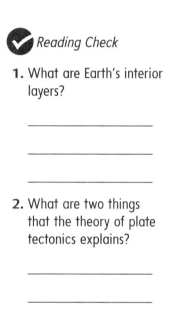 *Reading Check*

1. What are Earth's interior layers?

_____

_____

_____

2. What are two things that the theory of plate tectonics explains?

_____

_____

_____

The Theory of Plate Tectonics

The theory of plate tectonics states that the lithosphere (see below) is made up of huge, slowly moving rocky slabs called plates. The theory explains Earth processes such as the movement of the continents and the formation and occurrence of earthquakes, volcanoes, and mountains.

The Layers of Earth's Interior

Earth's interior is made up of three main layers.

- The crust is a thin layer of solid rock. The part under the oceans is called oceanic crust. The part under the continents is called continental crust.

- Most of the upper part of the mantle is solid rock. Most of the lower part of the mantle is also solid rock. Between the upper and lower parts of the mantle is a region that is partly melted, so it is able to flow.

- The outer part of the core is liquid. The inner part of the core is solid.

The Earth Layers That Are Important for Plate Tectonics

Together, Earth's crust and the upper part of the mantle are called the lithosphere. The lithosphere is solid rock.

The partly melted portion of the mantle is called the asthenosphere. The lithosphere floats on the asthenosphere.

Some of the Evidence for the Theory of Plate Tectonics

- The shape of the continents suggests that they were once joined together long ago as a single supercontinent. This huge land mass broke apart and its pieces (the continents) have been moving away from each other ever since. The continental drift hypothesis explains this idea.

- Evidence from sonar and other technologies shows that parts of the ocean floor are moving away from each other at mid-ocean ridges. New crust forms from lava erupting at these ridges. This process is called sea floor spreading. Continents are carried away from each other as part of this process.

Considering Evidence for Continental Drift

Use with textbook pages 284 and 285.

Read the information below, and answer the questions in the spaces provided.

Alfred Wegener noticed that the continents look like their coastlines match up like puzzle pieces. He hypothesized that all the continents were joined together long ago as a huge land mass called Pangaea. He suggested that Pangaea broke apart about 200 million years ago. The pieces of this land mass, which we know today as our continents, have been moving away from each other ever since.

This continental drift hypothesis depended on more than just the shape and fit of the continents. Wegener collected other kinds of evidence to support his ideas.

Fossil Evidence

Fossils of the reptile *Mesosaurus* have been found on two continents. *Mesosaurus* lived in fresh water and on land. It probably could not swim the great distance between continents. Fossils of other extinct organisms, *Lystrosaurus* and *Glossopteris*, also appear on different continents.

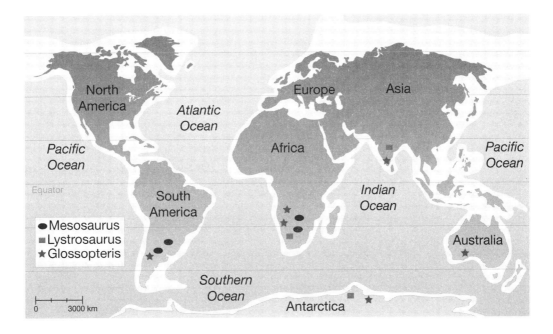

1. Why would Wegener have been interested in the fossil evidence described and shown above? What do you think he was thinking?

_____

_____

_____

Rock Evidence

The Appalachian Mountains in eastern North America are made of the same kind of rock as a mountain range in Britain and Norway. There are similarities between rock found in Quebec and rock found in northern Britain. There are also similarities between rock found in South America and rock found in Africa.

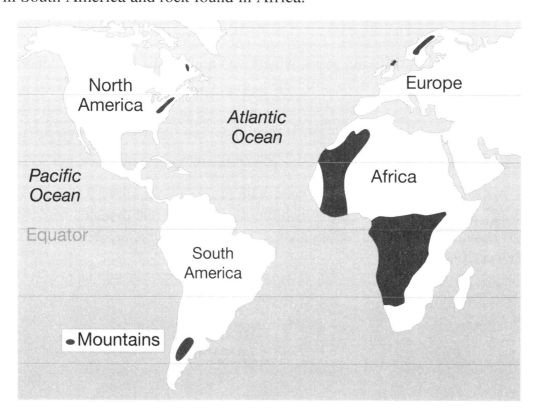

2. Why would Wegener have been interested in the rock evidence described and shown above? What do you think he was thinking?

_____

_____

_____

_____

Climate Evidence

In order for coal to form, there has to be lots of plant life in a tropical, swampy environment. When the plants die and are compressed under many layers of sediment for millions of years, coal is formed. Today, however coal deposits are found in moderate to cold environments. These include Canada, northern Europe, and Antarctica. Wegener also learned that some places that have warm environments today, such as Africa, India, and Australia, were partly covered long ago by glaciers.

3. What possible explanations are there for the information described above? What do you think Wegener was thinking?

_____

_____

_____

_____

Biological Evidence

Marsupials are mammals that are born before they develop completely. They continue to grow and develop in a pouch on their mother's body. Marsupials are found in Australia, North America, and South America. Kangaroos are examples of Australian marsupials. Opossums are North American marsupials.

Earthworms from the same biological families have been found on South America and Africa. Earthworms cannot swim and cannot survive the cold and salt of ocean water.

Similar kinds of coniferous trees are found in Australia, in South Africa, and in Brazil and Chile of South America.

4. What possible explanations are there for the information described above? What do you think Wegener was thinking?

_____

_____

_____

_____

Layers of Earth

Use with textbook page 277.

1. What is the difference between direct and indirect evidence?

_____

_____

2. Why was indirect evidence used to infer Earth's interior structure?

_____

_____

3. Why can we only infer details of the inner structure of Earth?

_____

_____

4. What was the indirect evidence used to infer Earth's layers?

_____

_____

5. Use the table to summarize the structure and composition of Earth's four layers.

Layer (Outside to Inside)	State (Solid or Liquid)	Description

Sea Floor Spreading

Use with textbook pages 278–280.

1. Sketch a graph that shows how the age of rock changes as you move away from the mid-ocean ridge in both directions.

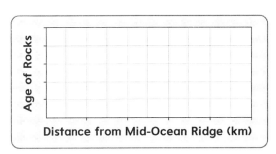

Age of Rocks

Distance from Mid-Ocean Ridge (km)

2. Sketch a graph that shows how the depth of sediment changes as you move away from the mid-ocean ridge in both directions.

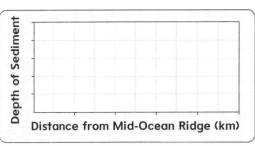

Depth of Sediment

Distance from Mid-Ocean Ridge (km)

3. How does the age of rocks at the mid-ocean ridge help explain how continents move?

_____

_____

4. How do changes in sediment depth at the mid-ocean ridge help explain how continents move?

_____

_____

5. The graph at right shows how heat (thermal energy) changes as it moves from below the crust at a mid-ocean ridge to the water surrounding the ridge. This change in the amount of heat is called heat flow. Interpret the graph. How does it help to explain what happens at a mid-ocean ridge?

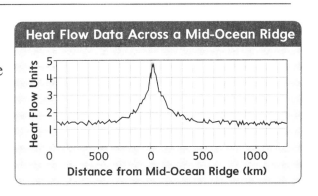

Heat Flow Data Across a Mid-Ocean Ridge

Heat Flow Units

5
4
3
2
1
0

0   500   0   500   1000

Distance from Mid-Ocean Ridge (km)

_____

_____

6. Summarize the process of sea floor spreading.

_____

_____

_____

4.1 Assessment

Match each term on the left with the best descriptor on the right. Each descriptor may be used only once.

Term	Descriptor
1. ____ asthenosphere	A. solid outer layer of Earth
2. ____ crust	B. molten rock from inside Earth
3. ____ mantle	C. partly melted part of the mantle
4. ____ outer core	D. deepest solid Earth layer
5. ____ inner core	E. solid Earth layer that is part of two other Earth layers
6. ____ lithosphere	F. deepest liquid Earth layer
7. ____ magma	G. Earth layer that has a portion that can flow

Circle the letter of the best answer for questions 8 to 18.

8. Which Earth process is explained by the theory of plate tectonics?

   A. climate   **C.** weathering

   B. mountain building   **D.** both B and C

9. Which of the following statements is true of the supercontinent Pangaea?

   A. Its existence would support the idea of "fixism."

   B. It sank into the ocean.

   C. It is believed to have existed about 200 million years ago.

   D. The present-day African continent was not a part of it.

10. Our scientific understanding of Earth's layers is based on

   A. analyzing how earthquake waves travel through Earth's interior

   B. inference

   C. indirect evidence

   D. all of the above

11. Earth's only liquid layer is called

   A. the crust   **C.** the mantle

   B. the outer core   **D.** the inner core

12. Identify the accurate statement(s).

    A. The theory of plate tectonics and the continental drift hypothesis are the same idea.

    B. The theory of plate tectonics includes the continental drift hypothesis.

    C. The continental drift hypothesis includes the theory of plate tectonics.

    D. A and C are both accurate.

13. The layer on which Earth's tectonic plates move is called

    A. the lithosphere

    B. the asthenosphere

    C. the mantle

    D. the crust

14. Earth's hottest layer is

    A. solid

    B. the outer core

    C. able to flow

    D. both B and C

15. Earth's thin, outer layer is called

    A. the crust

    B. the outer core

    C. the mantle

    D. the inner core

16. The age of ocean rocks as you move away from a mid-ocean ridge

    A. increases in both directions

    B. is constant

    C. decreases in both directions

    D. increases in one direction and decreases in the other

17. Sea floor spreading

    A. supports the idea that continents move

    B. explains how new oceanic crust is made

    C. occurs at a mid-ocean ridge

    D. all of the above are true

18. The theory of plate tectonics is a unifying theory because it explains

    A. how and why continents move

    B. why and where earthquakes occur

    C. how and why sea floor spreading occurs

    D. all of the above

19. Complete the graphic organizer below. Fill in examples from the Topic using key terms as well as your own words.

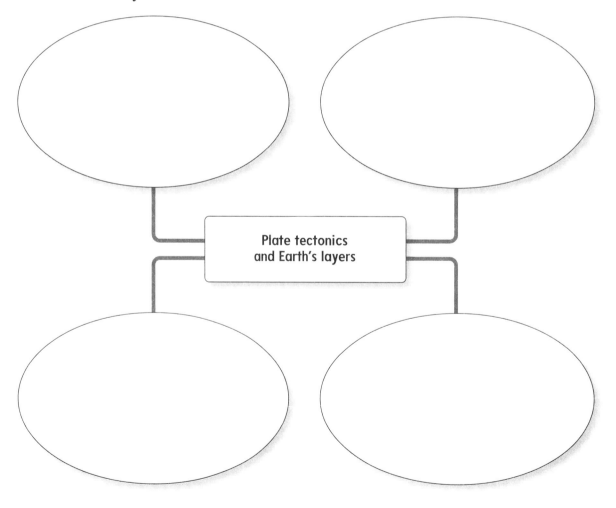

What are tectonic plates and how is their movement linked to geological processes?

Use with textbook pages 288-295.

Earth's Tectonic Plates

The lithosphere (Earth's crust and upper mantle) is broken into pieces called **tectonic plates**. They float on a part of the mantle called the asthenosphere, which can flow. Some tectonic plates are made up of oceanic crust. Most are made up of both oceanic crust and continental crust.

Plate Movement

When magma rises from an ocean ridge, the magma produces new crust, which pushes the plates apart. As these plates are pushed apart, other plates are pushed together. Movement along any plate boundary results in changes at other boundaries.

✔ *Reading Check*

What are the differences between the lithosphere and asthenosphere?

_____

_____

_____

Plate Movements

Plate Boundary	Motion of Plates	Activity and Features at Boundary	
Convergent	• plates move toward each other	• subduction (denser crust moves below less dense crust)	
		• deep ocean trenches	• volcanoes
		• mountains	• earthquakes
Divergent	• plates move apart	• formation of new oceanic crust	• sea floor spreading
		• mid-ocean ridges	• continental rifting
Transform	• plates slide past each other	• earthquakes	

Technologies such as the Global Positioning System (GPS) measure the rate at which tectonic plates move. Different plates move at rates that vary from 1 to 15 cm per year.

Mantle Convection

When partially melted mantle material is heated by Earth's core, it rises toward Earth's surface. Cooler, denser mantle material sinks away from the surface. This sets up large **convection currents** within the mantle. This **mantle convection** is thought to move tectonic plates. Two processes that result from mantle convection and contribute to tectonic plate movement are **ridge push** and **slab pull**. Ridge push occurs as rising material pushes plates apart. Slab pull occurs when a subducting plate pulls the rest of a plate down.

The Lithosphere and Asthenosphere

Use with textbook page 290.

1. Describe how the following terms are related:

   a) lithosphere and crust

   _____

   b) lithosphere and mantle

   _____

   c) asthenosphere and mantle

   _____

2. What is the key role of the asthenosphere in the theory of plate tectonics?

   _____

   _____

3. What characteristics of the asthenosphere make it suitable for moving Earth's tectonic plates?

   _____

   _____

4. One analogy compares the asthenosphere to toothpaste or melted tar. Come up with your own analogy to describe the asthenosphere.

   _____

5. Use the Venn diagram to compare and contrast continental and oceanic crust.

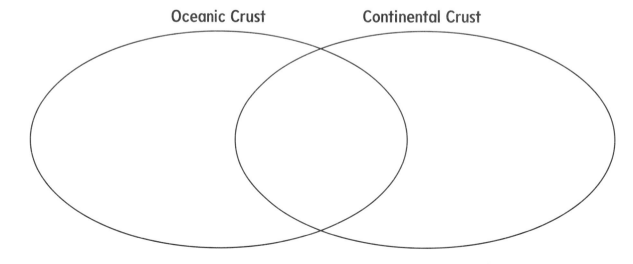

Oceanic Crust   **Continental Crust**

Plate Boundaries

Use with textbook pages 291–292.

1. Identify each type of plate boundary shown in the table, and describe the type of geological activity that occurs at that boundary.

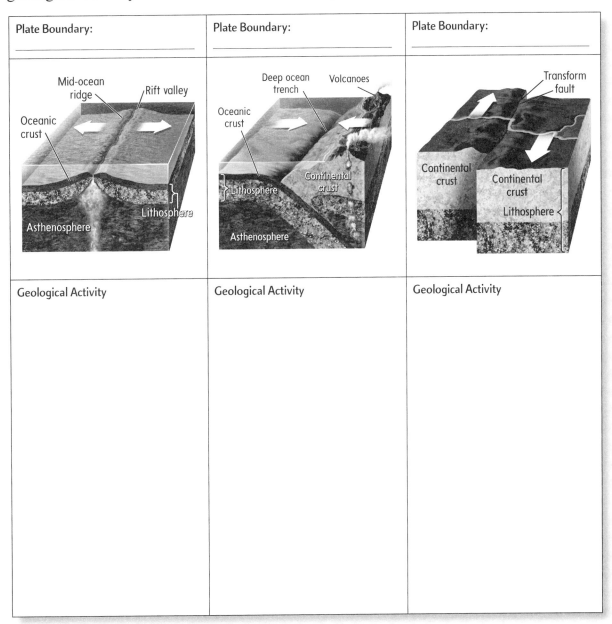

Plate Boundary: _____	Plate Boundary: _____	Plate Boundary: _____
Geological Activity	Geological Activity	Geological Activity

2. Use your understanding of divergent and convergent plate boundaries to explain why the surface of Earth is not getting any larger or smaller.

_____

_____

Mantle Convection

Use with textbook page 294.

1. What two sources supply the heat energy that drives mantle convection?

   _____

2. How could you use a hot plate, a large beaker, water, and food colouring to model mantle convection? Draw a diagram to show what your model would look like, and explain how your model represents convection in Earth's mantle.

   _____

   _____

   _____

4.2 Assessment

Match each geological feature or process on the left with the plate boundary or boundaries it is associated with on the right. A geological feature or process can be present at more than one type of plate boundary.

Geological Feature or Process	Plate Boundary
1. _____ subduction	A. divergent plate boundary
2. _____ plate separation	B. convergent plate boundary
3. _____ mountain formation	C. transform plate boundary
4. _____ creation of new crust	
5. _____ plates sliding past one another	
6. _____ plate collision	
7. _____ deep sea trenches	
8. _____ volcanoes	
9. _____ mid-ocean ridge	
10. _____ earthquakes	
11. _____ continental rifting	
12. _____ sea floor spreading	

Circle the letter of the best answer for questions 13 to 24.

13. Which of the following best describes the lithosphere?

    A. It comprises of only the crust.

    B. It comprises of only mantle material.

    C. It comprises of crust and part of the upper mantle.

    D. It comprises of parts of all of Earth's layers.

14. Which of the following best describes the asthenosphere?

    A. The material that makes up tectonic plates.

    B. A material that flows.

    C. Partially melted crust.

    D. Liquid outer core.

15. Which statement best describes the relationship between the lithosphere and asthenosphere?

   A. The lithosphere and asthenosphere are fused (joined) together.

   B. The lithosphere and asthenosphere do not interact.

   C. The asthenosphere floats on the lithosphere.

   D. The lithosphere is broken into tectonic plates that float on the asthenosphere.

16. At a divergent plate boundary,

   A. subduction occurs

   B. sea floor spreading occurs

   C. plates collide

   D. deep sea trenches form

17. At a convergent plate boundary,

   A. subduction occurs

   B. rifts are present

   C. plates move apart

   D. new oceanic crust is made

18. At a transform plate boundary,

   A. subduction occurs

   B. there are volcanoes

   C. plates slide past each other

   D. mid-ocean ridges form

19. Deep sea trenches

   A. form at subduction zones

   B. form at convergent plate boundaries

   C. are the deepest parts of the oceans

   D. All of the statements are correct

20. Subduction occurs

    A. when plates slide past each other

    B. when tectonic plates are not moving

    C. at mid-ocean ridges

    D. when dense crust goes below less dense crust

21. The movement of tectonic plates

    A. can be measured using satellites

    B. is measured in cm/year

    C. causes plates to interact

    D. All of the statements are correct

22. Which statement best describes convection?

    A. Cool fluid rises, while warm fluid sinks.

    B. Warm fluid stays at the surface, while cool fluid stays at the bottom.

    C. Warm fluid rises, while cool fluid sinks.

    D. Cool fluid stays at the surface, while warm fluid stays at the bottom.

23. Which statement best describes slab pull?

    A. Occurs at subduction zones.

    B. Leading edge of plate pulls rest of plate down.

    C. Gravity assists with plate movement.

    D. All of the statements are correct.

24. Which statement best describes ridge push?

    A. Occurs where convection is moving mantle material down.

    B. Occurs at convergent plate boundaries.

    C. Pushes tectonic plates apart.

    D. All of the statements are correct.

25. Use a graphic organizer like the one below, or another of your choosing, to compare and contrast the three types of plate boundaries.

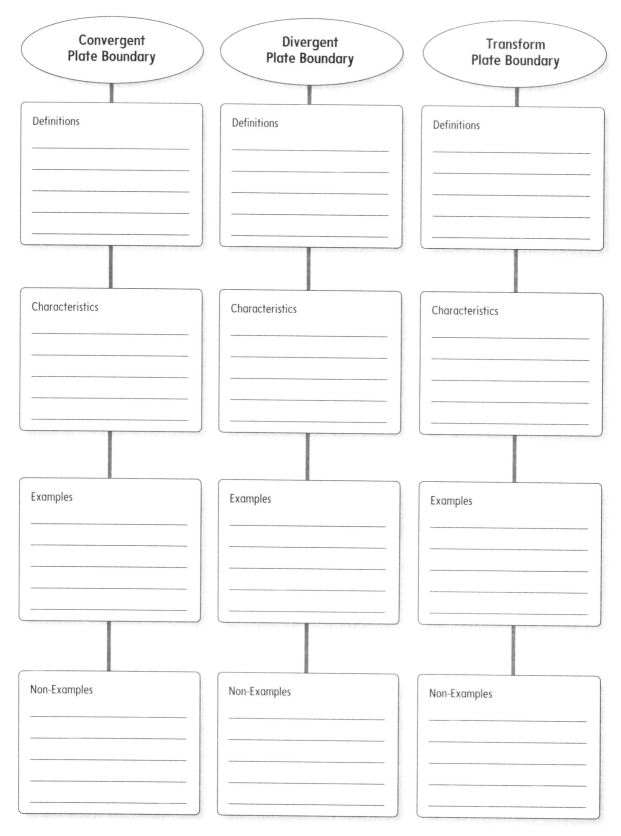

How does the theory of plate tectonics explain Earth's geological processes?

Use with textbook pages 298–313.

Earthquakes

Almost all **earthquakes** occur at tectonic plate boundaries. The movement of the plates applies pressure to rock. When the pressure is too great, the rock breaks and the energy is released in the form of an earthquake. A **fault** is the surface along which rocks break and move. The three types of faults are summarized in the table below.

The place deep in the crust where an earthquake starts is called the focus. The surface location directly above the focus is called the epicentre. As an earthquake occurs, vibrations called seismic waves are released.

Seismographs are used to measure and record ground movement. Data from seismographs can be used to determine strength and location of an earthquake. The Richter scale is used to represent the **magnitude** or strength of an earthquake. An increase of 1 on the scale represents a 10-fold increase in the strength of the earthquake.

 Summarize

Write a short paragraph that summarizes the relationship among a fault, a focus, and an epicentre.

Types of Faults

Reverse	• rock is squeezed together • one block rides up and over the other block • crust is shortened	
Normal	• rock is pulled apart • one block slips down relative to the other block • crust is lengthened	
Strike-slip	• blocks of rock move past each other horizontally	

✓ *Reading Check*

What is the difference between magma and lava?

_____

_____

_____

Volcanoes

Magma moves from the mantle to Earth's surface at **volcanoes**. When magma reaches the surface of Earth it is referred to as lava.

Volcanoes can occur at oceanic-oceanic or oceanic-continental convergent plate boundaries. When an oceanic plate is subducted beneath another plate, magma can rise to form volcanoes. An oceanic trench forms where an oceanic plate is subducted. A curved group of volcanic islands forms when an oceanic plate subducts beneath another oceanic plate. High mountain ranges form when an oceanic plate subducts beneath a continental plate.

Mountain Ranges

Mountain ranges form at convergent plate boundaries. At oceanic-continental convergent boundaries volcanic mountains form as well as mountain ranges produced from pressure from colliding plates. At continental-continental plate boundaries, there is no subduction. This means one plate is pushed up on the other forming mountains. This is how the Himalayan mountain range is thought to have formed.

At the Surface: Before and After

Use with textbook pages 300-301.

1. Draw a cross-section or aerial view that shows what an area of land looks like before and after an earthquake occurs along a normal fault.

2. Draw a cross-section or aerial view that shows what an area of land looks like before and after an earthquake occurs along a strike-slip fault.

3. Draw a cross-section or aerial view that shows what an area of land looks like before and after an earthquake occurs along a reverse fault.

Interpreting Epicentres of the Juan de Fuca Plate

Use with textbook pages 300–301.

There is a usually an earthquake of very low magnitude (strength) every day in B.C. Most of these earthquakes originate beneath the ocean floor. Some have their focus in the crust at depths of 20 km or less. Major earthquakes occur within the Juan de Fuca plate and the subduction zone shown in the diagram below. Only earthquakes larger than magnitude 4 are shown. (Earthquakes of magnitude 4 will be felt by most people but are unlikely to cause much damage. Magnitude 5 and higher earthquakes have damaging effects.)

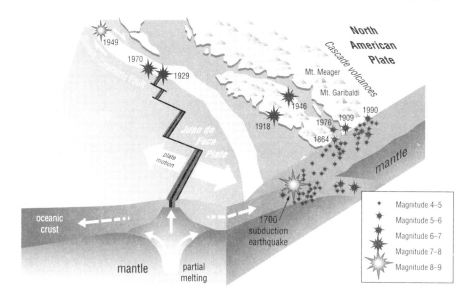

Write a paragraph to answer this question: Why do you think there are so many earthquakes in this area? Your answer should be based on evidence from the diagram and your understanding of plate tectonics.

_____

_____

_____

_____

_____

_____

_____

_____

_____

_____

Volcanoes at Convergent Boundaries

Use with textbook pages 306–307.

1. Explain how volcanoes form at convergent plate boundaries.

_____

_____

_____

2. What characteristic of the converging plates determines which plate is subducted? You may wish to refer back to Topic 4.2 in your textbook, if necessary.

_____

3. List the hazards that volcanoes can present.

_____

_____

_____

4. Use the Venn diagram to compare the geologic features at the two types of oceanic convergent boundaries.

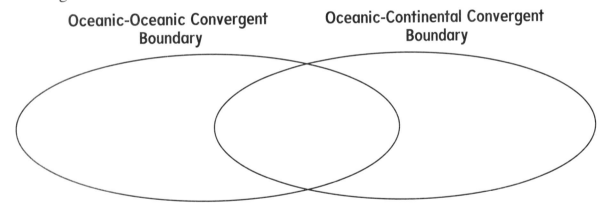

Oceanic-Oceanic Convergent Boundary   **Oceanic-Continental Convergent Boundary**

5. Why do islands form at an oceanic-oceanic convergent plate boundary?

_____

_____

6. Why do mountain ranges form at an oceanic-continental convergent plate boundary?

_____

_____

Volcanic Ash Analysis

An erupting volcano can produce huge clouds of ash that extend hundreds of kilometres. The ash can cause breathing problems as well as damage to crops, buildings, and machinery. The map at right shows deposits of volcanic ash in western North America over a long period of time. Use the map to answer the questions that follow.

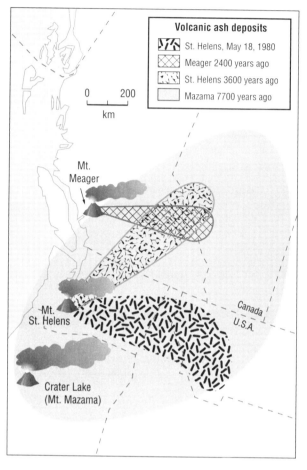

Volcanic ash deposits
- St. Helens, May 18, 1980
- Meager 2400 years ago
- St. Helens 3600 years ago
- Mazama 7700 years ago

Mt. Meager

Mt. St. Helens

Crater Lake (Mt. Mazama)

Canada U.S.A.

0   200
km

1. Which volcano created the largest expanse of ash? When did it happen?

_____

_____

2. What direction do you think the wind was blowing when the volcanoes erupted? What evidence are you using to make your inference?

_____

_____

_____

3. Why are cities in the interior of B.C. more likely than coastal cities to receive ash from the volcanoes shown?

_____

_____

_____

Mountain Ranges

Use with textbook pages 307, 309, and 310.

1. Why do colliding continental plates behave differently than an oceanic plate colliding with a continental plate?

   _____

   _____

   _____

2. Why is there no volcanic activity at a continental-continental convergent boundary?

   _____

   _____

   _____

3. Explain the differences between the formation of the Coast Mountains in British Columbia and the Himalayan Mountains in southern Asia.

   _____

   _____

   _____

4. The Burgess Shale is famous for its fossils. It is located 2286 m above sea level in Yoho National Park near Golden, British Columbia. It contains 508-million-year-old fossils of sea organisms that lived on a reef. Use plate tectonics to explain how fossils of sea creatures can be found high in the mountains.

   _____

   _____

   _____

5. What plates collided (and are still colliding) and resulted in the formation of the Himalayan Mountains?

   _____

   _____

4.3 Assessment

Match each term on the left with the best descriptor on the right. Each descriptor may be used only once.

Term	Descriptor
1. _____ focus	A. earthquake vibrations
2. _____ seismograph	B. anywhere that molten rock from the mantle reaches Earth's surface
3. _____ reverse fault	C. occurs when blocks of rock are squeezed together
4. _____ earthquake	D. seismic waves that move the fastest
5. _____ hot spot volcano	E. occurs when blocks of rock slide past each other
6. _____ fault	F. seismic waves that only travel on the surface of Earth
7. _____ epicentre	G. point on Earth's surface directly above where earthquake starts
8. _____ seismic waves	H. natural movement of the ground when part of Earth's crust shifts
9. _____ subduction	I. occurs when blocks of rock are pulled apart
10. _____ strike-slip fault	J. seismic waves that can only travel through solids
11. _____ surface waves	K. location on Earth where earthquake starts
12. _____ normal fault	L. instrument that measures and records ground vibrations
13. _____ secondary waves	M. used to measure the magnitude of earthquakes
14. _____ volcano	N. the break in rock where movement happens during an earthquake
15. _____ primary waves	O. the movement of one tectonic plate under another
16. _____ Richter scale	P. occurs away from plate boundaries

Circle the letter of the best answer for questions 17 to 27.

17. Which of the following statements describe earthquakes?

    A. Earthquakes can be predicted.

    B. Most earthquakes occur at tectonic plate boundaries.

    C. Earthquakes only occur under the oceans.

    D. All of the statements are correct.

Use the table to answer questions 18 to 20.

I	strike-slip fault
II	reverse fault
III	normal fault

18. Which types of faults can form due to an earthquake?

    A. I and II

    B. I and III

    C. II and III

    D. I, II, and III

19. Which types of faults result in vertical (up or down) movement of blocks of rock?

    A. I

    B. I and II

    C. II and III

    D. I, II, and III

20. Which types of faults result in only horizontal movement of blocks of rock?

    A. I

    B. I and II

    C. II and III

    D. I, II, and III

21. Which statement best describes the epicentre of an earthquake?

    A. The point where breakage of rock first happens.

    B. The break where movement happens.

    C. The point on Earth's surface directly above the focus.

    D. All of the above statements are true.

22. Which statement best describes primary (P) waves?

    A. Travel only through solids.

    B. Cause rock particles to move forward and backward.

    C. Slowest of the three types of waves.

    D. All of the above statements are true.

23. Which statement best describes secondary (S) waves?

    A. Travel only through solids.

    B. Fastest of the three types of waves.

    C. Cause rock particles to move up and down and side to side.

    D. All of the above statements are true.

24. Which statement best describes surface (L) waves?

    A. Travel only along the surface of Earth.

    B. Slowest of the three types of waves.

    C. Often cause the greatest damage.

    D. All of the above statements are true.

25. When an oceanic plate collides with another tectonic plate,

    A. subduction occurs.

    B. an oceanic trench is formed.

    C. magma can rise to the surface and cause an eruption.

    D. All of the above statements are true.

26. Which statement best describes a hot spot volcano?

    A. They form at tectonic plate boundaries.

    B. They show evidence of tectonic plate movement.

    C. They occur due to subduction.

    D. All of the above statements are true.

27. When two continental plates collide,

    A. subduction occurs.

    B. mountain ranges form.

    C. volcanoes are formed.

    D. the plates stop moving.

28. Use the table to show how plate tectonics can be used to explain the occurrences of earthquakes, volcanoes, and mountain formation.

Geological Process	Explanation
Earthquakes	
Volcanoes	
Mountain Formation	

How do geological features and processes affect where and how we live?

Use with textbook pages 318-325.

Summarize

What have you and your family done to prepare for a natural disaster?

_____

_____

_____

British Columbia's Landscape

Geological processes have shaped B.C.'s landscape and given rise to features such as mineral deposits, river deltas, and hot springs. These features have influenced settlement patterns over the long history of the province.

Region	Geological Features
Northern Interior	• glacial lakes • nutrient rich soils • jade deposits in ancient oceanic rock
Northeast Peace River Region	• rich soils from ancient glacial lake • natural gas, oil and coal deposits • fossils
Southern Interior	• steep-walled canyons • lakes • mineral resources
Rocky Mountains	• some of Canada's highest mountains • North America's longest mountain valley • hot springs
Coastal Regions	• mountains and islands • earthquakes • dormant volcanoes

Geohazards

Geohazards are destructive events that result from geological processes. The province is vulnerable to many types of geohazards due to factors such as its location near active tectonic plate boundaries, the amount of rain and snow that falls, and the effects of ancient glaciers.

When and where earthquakes and other geohazards occur cannot be predicted accurately. Individuals, families, and governments can take steps to be more prepared for any type of geohazard.

Being Prepared

Use with textbook pages 323–324.

1. Even though we are unable to predict when a particular geohazard such as an earthquake will occur, it is important to be prepared for such an event. List all of the items you think should be kept in an emergency preparedness kit.

   _____

   _____

   _____

2. Visit the City of Vancouver website and review what is recommended for an evacuation kit and a home emergency preparedness kit. Write down any items you did not include on your list in question #1.

   _____

   _____

3. Tofino and Vancouver are both located near the Cascadia subduction zone. People in both places need to be prepared for the high likelihood of an earthquake occurring. However, the people of Tofino need to be prepared for different geohazards than the people of Vancouver.

   a) Find the District of Tofino and the City of Vancouver on a map. If an earthquake occurred off the west coast of British Columbia, what type of resulting geohazard would Tofino residents need to be prepared for that Vancouver residents would not?

   _____

   b) Why would this particular geohazard be a risk for Tofino, but not Vancouver?

   _____

   _____

4. Governments have a responsibility to ensure residents are aware of the risks of geohazards in their region and how to prepare for them.

   a) What does your local government do to inform residents of geohazard risks and how to prepare for them?

   _____

   b) What does the provincial government do?

   _____

Geohazards in British Columbia

Use with textbook pages 322–323.

British Columbia is vulnerable to different types of geohazards.

1. Briefly describe some of the geohazards to which British Columbia is vulnerable.

_____

_____

2. a) What factors make British Columbia vulnerable to geohazards?

_____

_____

b) Which of these factors might also make British Columbia an attractive place for people to live? Explain.

_____

_____

_____

3. British Columbia is Canada's most tectonically active province.

a) Which tectonic plates contribute to British Columbia's geohazard risk?

_____

_____

b) What type of tectonic plate boundaries exist near British Columbia?

_____

_____

_____

c) What geohazards do these tectonic plate interactions put British Columbia at risk of?

_____

_____

_____

The Geology of Your Region

Use with textbook pages 320–323.

1. Identify on the map the region where you live.

_____

Northwest

Northeast

Central Interior

Central Coast

Kootenay

Southern Interior

Vancouver Island

Lower Mainland   Okanagan Boundary

2. Think about the landforms and other geologic features of the place where you live.

a) What geologic features makes your local area attractive to you?

_____

_____

b) What geologic features make your local area attractive to tourists?

_____

_____

3. What geohazards could occur in your region?

_____

_____

4. Research the geological history of your local area.

a) How has the geological history given rise to the geologic features you enjoy?

_____

_____

_____

b) How has the geological history contributed to the risk of geohazards in your region?

_____

_____

_____

4.4 Assessment

Match the geohazards with their associated effects. Each effect may be associated with more than one geohazard.

Effect	Geohazard
1. movement of snow down a mountainside	A. volcano
2. can release large amounts of ash into atmosphere	B. earthquake
3. can cause damage to roads/bridges	C. avalanche
4. can give rise to tsunamis	D. mud/landslide
5. releases molten rock	
6. movement of mud down a mountainside	
7. violent shaking of ground	
8. can melt snow/glaciers causing lahars (mudslides)	

Circle the letter of the best answer for questions 9 to 14.

9. Which of the following statements is true of geohazards?

A. They can pose threats to people and property.

B. They are always human caused.

C. They only happen in the winter.

D. They can be predicted.

10. What region of Canada has the greatest amount of earthquake activity?

A. Saskatchewan   **C.** Central Ontario

B. Western British Columbia   **D.** Nunavut

11. Why does British Columbia have a history of volcanic activity?

A. It is located near the Pacific Ocean.   **C.** It is a mountainous region.

B. It has many deep valleys.   **D.** It is near tectonic plate boundaries.

12. Which of the following statements is not true of earthquakes?

A. They can give rise to tsunamis.

B. They usually occur at tectonic plate boundaries.

C. They can be accurately predicted.

D. British Columbia is at risk of earthquakes.

13. Which of the reasons could be used to explain why British Columbia is susceptible to geohazards?

    A. It has substantial amounts of snow and rain.

    B. It is a mountainous province.

    C. It is located in a tectonically active region.

    D. All of the reasons could be used.

14. The presence of tectonic plate boundaries near British Columbia

    A. puts British Columbia at greater risk of geohazards.

    B. explains the presence of volcanoes in British Columbia.

    C. explains why British Columbia is at high risk of earthquakes.

    D. All of the above statements are true.

15. Complete the mind map for British Columbia's geological processes and their effects on the landscape and communities.

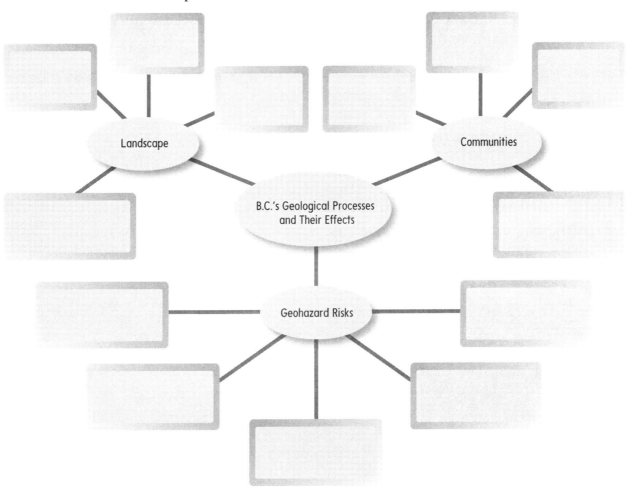

Should we worry about the Cascadia subduction zone?

What's the Issue?

The Cascadia subduction zone stretches from Vancouver Island to northern California. It is believed that the subduction zone is overdue for a megathrust earthquake. The west coast of North America, which parallels the subduction zone, is home to more than 10 million people who live in the "hazard zone." Large cities near the subduction zone include Vancouver, British Columbia; Seattle, Washington; and Portland, Oregon. Geologists have used scientific research as well as traditional oral narratives from coastal First Peoples to piece together the geologic history of the region. This history shows evidence of past megathrust earthquakes.

Other regions that have characteristics similar to the Cascadia subduction zone and have experienced megathrust earthquakes include northern Japan and Indonesia. In 2004 the Indian Ocean earthquake off the coast of Indonesia resulted in 230 000 to 280 000 deaths, and in 2011 the Tohoku earthquake off the coast of Japan resulted in more than 15 000 deaths.

Dig Deeper

Collaborate with your classmates to explore one or more of these questions—or generate your own questions to explore.

1. The Cascadia subduction zone is located at convergent plate boundaries.

   a) What tectonic plates form the Cascadia subduction zone?

   b) What geologic features typical of a convergent plate boundary can be found near the subduction zone?

2. The Cascade volcanic arc extends from north of Whistler, British Columbia, through the states of Washington and Oregon and into northern California.

   a) List the volcanoes that belong to this volcanic arc.

   b) What major eruptions have occurred along the arc?

   c) Use the theory of plate tectonics to explain the existence of these volcanoes.

3. It is believed that the last megathrust earthquake to occur on the subduction zone happened in 1700.

   a) What is the Neskowin Ghost Forest and how was it used to show evidence of the 1700 earthquake?

   b) What coastal First Peoples have traditional oral narratives that include the stories of the 1700 earthquake?

   c) What evidence for the 1700 earthquake has been found in British Columbia?

4. Earthquakes that occur at underwater subduction zones can cause devastating tsunamis.

   a) How and why does a tsunami form?

   b) What have coastal communities along the subduction zone done to prepare for a potential tsunami?

   c) What areas of British Columbia are especially at risk of a tsunami?

5. Geologists believe the Cascadia subduction zone is overdue for a high magnitude megathrust earthquake.

   a) What evidence has been collected to suggest the region is due for an earthquake?

   b) If a megathrust earthquake were to happen, what geohazards could occur?

   c) What have the various levels of government in British Columbia done to prepare for a future megathrust earthquake?

Notes:

Notes: